Red Dust and Rainforests

*Cannibals, Cassowaries and ill-fated adventurers:
a motorcycle adventure through the tropics of
Queensland to the tip of Australia-Cape York*

Gary Wood

 A catalogue record for this book is available from the National Library of Australia

Copyright © 2025 by Gary Wood

All rights reserved; no part of this book may be reproduced or used in any manner, including the right to reproduce this book or portions thereof in any form without the written permission of the copyright owner.

This book is non-fiction.

Publisher: Digital Swaggie Publishing
Email: gary@digitalswaggie.com.au

National Library of Australia Prepublication Data Service

Author: Gary Wood

Title: **Red Dust and Rainforests**

Cannibals, Cassowaries and ill-fated adventurers: A motorcycle adventure through the tropics of Queensland to the tip of Australia-Cape York.

Genre: Travel and Adventure

ISBN: 978-1-7635631-3-1 (Paperback)
ISBN: 978-1-7635631-4-8 (Hard Copy)
ISBN: 978-1-7635631-5-5 (e-book)

Table of Contents

Chapter 1: Adventure Calling Again 5

Chapter 2: An Unexpected Opportunity...8

Chapter 3: Back to the Beach..10

Chapter 4: Bowen - The Beginning of North Queensland..................15

Chapter 5: Sarina to Townsville 17

Chapter 6: Free Beach Camping..22

Chapter 7: Kokomo in North Queensland 27

Chapter 8: The Funniest Toilet in Queensland....................................32

Chapter 9: German-Speaking Crocodiles Again 35

Chapter 10: Opium, Slavery and Ill-fated Adventurers 41

Chapter 11: Murder and Cannibalism 45

Chapter 12: Cairns and a snub to Captain Cook 49

Chapter 13: The Daintree: The Oldest Rainforest in the World...........54

Chapter 14: Encounter with a Cassowary 58

Chapter 15: A Biker's Right of Passage 63

Chapter 16: An Evil Mountain 66

Chapter 17: Cook's Town and the Journey Home 69

Chapter 18: Learning to Ride in the Mud 87
Chapter 19: Camping at the Waterpark 92
Chapter 20: Riding Mud 96
Chapter 21: Journey to the Northernmost Tip of Australia:
  Cape York 111
Chapter 22: The Journey Begins 115
Chapter 23: The Peninsula Development Road (PDR) 119
Chapter 24: Corrugations and Bulldust 122
Chapter 25: The Road Less Travelled 129
Chapter 26: The Northern Tip of the Australian Continent 138
Chapter 27: The Journey Home 143
Chapter 28: The Lion's Den Hotel 151
Chapter 29: A New Beginning 154
Chapter 30: What Have I Learnt? 155
Chapter 31: The End of the Beginning 158

Prologue

My life changed after my first ride around Central and Southern Queensland. I had come back to my familiar world with a new sense of freedom. The feelings of dissociation I felt in my old life were no longer there. I had developed a renewed love for exploration and adventure. I had set a new goal, but had no idea how I was going to achieve it.

The challenge ahead is riding one of Australia's most remote roads that leads to the northernmost tip of the Australian continent, Cape York. If you ride an adventure motorcycle or are an adventurer looking for a different experience, you can't look past Far North Queensland.

It will be one of your life's most exciting adventures. It's a "Nirvana" for adventure motorcycle riders. It has it all: rough dirt roads, creek crossings, lonely outback highways, and stories of ill-fated adventurers and pioneers. It boasts tranquil tropical beaches, a lush rainforest, and the Great Barrier Reef as its backdrop. The Daintree is the oldest rainforest in the world, protected by the aggressive giant birds known as cassowaries. The Queensland tropics are one of the most diverse ecosystems in the world.

But it's not without its difficulties; there are steep rainforest tracks and long, dusty roads with torturous bulldust pits all too willing to catch the unwary traveller. The river and creek crossings are treacherous, with giant crocodiles in every waterhole. There are spiders as big as dinner plates and at least five of the most deadly snakes in the world, including the mythical and elusive "Hoop Snake." But these adrenaline-charged experiences are the adventure. As they say, it's not the destination but the journey that matters.

In "Red Dust and Rainforests," I continue my quest to visit every accessible beach in Queensland and to find the best one. But deep down in my conscious mind is the one bucket list item above all others that drives me: Cape York and the small sign concreted to the tiny, sometimes submerged, rock escarpment that says, "You are standing on the northernmost point of the Australian continent - Cape York."

I travel through the Queensland tropics, camp on lonely tropical beaches, and visit the site where adventurers before me met their end through cannibalism and hostile Aborigines. I cross crocodile-infested rivers—sometimes travelling solo, at other times with like-minded companions. Throughout my travels, I build on my list of "WoW factors" and "Moments." These are the jewels in my travel; they take my breath away and make me appreciate the simplicity and beauty of nature. I reflect on the joy of travelling with fellow riders and the bond that adversity creates. It's one that only fellow adventurers with the same dreams can understand.

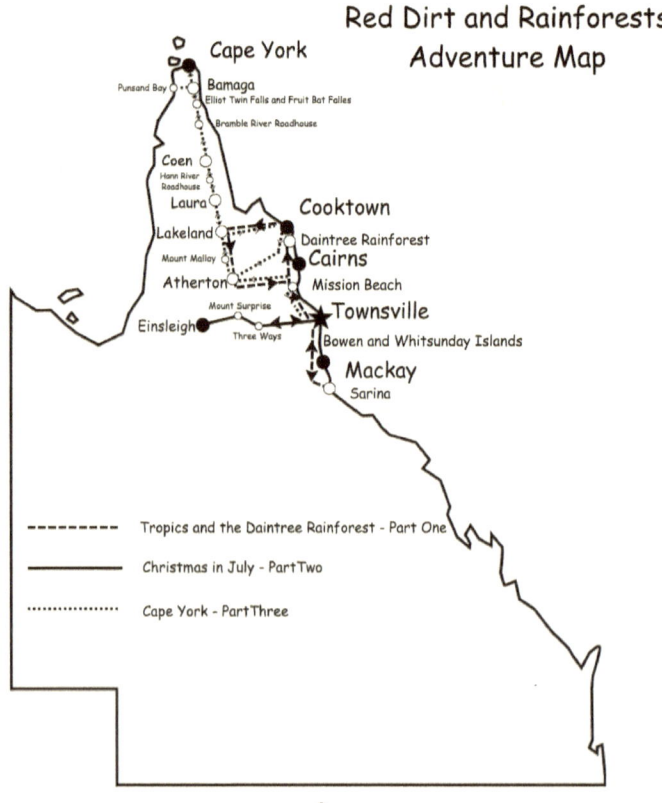

Chapter 1
Adventure Calling Again

A storm is brewing out the back of the Great Dividing Range. I can feel the moisture in the air, which is common in the tropics during the summer, but this time, there's electricity charging the air particles. The hairs on my neck are alive with energy as a large bolt of fork lightning crashes down, pulverising the land less than five kilometres from where I'm relaxing in my hammock. It's an incredible display of the raw power of nature. I'm getting a little nervous about lying here with such raw power so close.

Since returning from my thirty-day ride around Queensland, I've been more attuned to the environment. Electrical storms make me feel alive; the raw power of Mother Nature is impossible to comprehend. It's one of those "WoW" factors that takes your breath away and helps you realise your place in this extraordinary world. Discovering new facts about a place and experiencing the beauty of nature is what makes adventure travel a wonderful experience.

Now, as I sit watching the fury of Mother Nature, I'm drawn back to the road. I want to continue what I started all those years ago: adventure was calling. It's like a bottle of champagne, dormant until someone pops the cork and the contents spray out under pressure. Contrary to its sophisticated image of refinement, the sweet, sticky wine becomes uncontrollable. It's a metaphor for the raw chaos of life; its natural state is wild and free until we contain it in carefully crafted crystal glasses. (There are other metaphors I could use, but this is a family book.)

During my first solo motorcycle tour of Queensland, I set in place this desire to ride to Cape York, the northernmost tip of the Australian continent. At the time, it seemed too far away and too complicated for a beginner. However, I now feel it is achievable, and it has become my driving desire.

In my book "Gun Fights, Ghosts and Goannas", I discuss the movie, "City Slickers" and "Smiley's: One-finger Salute to the Meaning of Life." I can now hold my finger in the air and say, "I know what Smiley meant." If you haven't seen the movie "City Slickers, I suggest you do. It epitomises the feelings of being lost and not knowing what direction to take in life.

I was in the same place about three years ago when a song came over my speakers that reminded me of a dream I had. It inspired me to buy a motorcycle and set off on a solo adventure around Queensland. My motorcycle is a KLR 650 dual sport, and he goes by the name of Emu. Together, we rode over eight thousand kilometres around Queensland. By the time this next adventure is complete, I will have ridden over twenty thousand kilometres.

Another clap of thunder is followed by a thick flash of fork lightning even closer than the last. The storm will be directly overhead in a minute; I sit under the eaves of my house watching the fireworks and feeling the rumble and roar of the thunder. The rain is pounding all around me. Ordinarily, I would retreat inside the house, but I feel safe here; it's like I'm somehow connected to everything happening around me.

I'm once again in my hammock, contemplating my next adventure. It has been over six months since I returned, and I feel more at peace with the world than I have for a long time. Maybe even since I was drinking at Fisherman's Wharf on the Gold Coast and heard that song played by the band all those years ago.

Life was easier and the possibilities endless back then. I reflect on my previous journey and the distances I will travel to achieve my next bucket list items. My quest is still to travel around Australia. This next adventure will be one more piece of that puzzle. But I must complete the Queensland section and continue with what I started. I have already documented almost every accessible beach on the Queensland Coast from Coolangatta to Clearview near Sarina.

There's still half the coastline to see and salt air to taste. As I sit and watch Mother Nature display her power, I become perplexed and anxious; I'm unsure how to balance this with my work commitments.

It might have stayed a dream if I had not prioritised it and started thinking through the endless possibilities to make it happen. I'm unsure if it was the adrenaline I was experiencing, being so close to nature's fury, or the realisation I had made a new goal. But now I felt emboldened, so I began to create a list of items, starting with a ride as far up the coast of Queensland as possible and a mission to explore its renowned tropical beaches.

If my mind stays focused on this goal, the universe will find a way to make it happen. I've committed to riding to the northernmost tip of the Australian continent.

As the days march on, I'm becoming increasingly obsessed with the thought of the adventurous journey. A fervent passion, almost bordering on obsession, has been ignited.

Is the universe eavesdropping on my thoughts? No sooner did this obsession take hold than an opportunity to take time away from work arose. I seize the moment and make plans to continue my adventure.

Chapter 2
An Unexpected Opportunity

My desire to visit and write about all the beaches arose from a blog post I wrote back when I started my blog Digital Swaggie in 2019. I wrote that Bowen has the best beaches in Queensland. One of my readers challenged me, "How do you know? Have you been to them all?" Good point, I thought, no, but I should. Now, I'm on a quest to visit as many beaches as possible and develop a top twelve list.

Queensland has some of the best beaches in Australia (maybe I shouldn't say that because I haven't been to them all), and I intend to see as many of them as possible. I also want to get back on the road and explore more of Queensland on another adventure. Summer isn't the best season to ride in the tropics; it is wet, and the humidity is oppressive. It's not so bad riding, but camping in the tropics during summer is uncomfortable; the hot stickiness and the lack of breeze conspire to prevent you from sleeping deeply, and, consequently, you often wake up tired and lacking energy. This is where a good strong cup of coffee comes in.

Over the past six months, I've been lamenting on how I can improve my riding experience. It is clear that I also need to upgrade Emu's capacity to handle deep bulldust roads and river crossings. The KLR650 is an excellent adventure bike, but it has limitations in the standard configuration. For one thing, the bloody seat is the most uncomfortable seat I have ever sat on, so it was the first item to be replaced.

After spending a month or two online and discussing the various options, I couldn't find the answers in the online forums. Eventually, I settled on a Sargent's seat made in the USA. It took a month to get the seat to North Queensland. While expensive, it is worth the money as I wanted something with a reputation for comfort, and Sargent's are well known for producing comfortable seats.

The tyres are worn out from the first 8,000 kilometres around Queensland and need replacing. Again, I spend hours on Facebook forums trying to find the best options. Eventually, I took the advice of the Kawasaki shop mechanic.

In the end, I decide on some off-road knobbys. I reason the most dangerous stuff is off-road riding, there being plenty of red bulldust where I am going. Therefore, having the best off-road tyres made sense. I place a Dunlop D605 on the back and a D603 on the front. While Emu is getting a service, I have a Yoshimura exhaust fitted. The new exhaust not only sounded mean, it also makes Emu breathe easier and gives him more low-end power.

He is punchier at the lights; Emu has gone from a low-level "put put put" to a roaring lion that makes people turn and look. I'm sure he would have felt a surge in his self-esteem if he was human; I could imagine a puffed-out chest and a bounce in his stride. Other modifications include new foot pegs to prevent slipping off when it rains and a KLR Dash kit to raise the windscreen and reduce wind noise.

Riding from Salvator Rosa in my first adventure, I noticed the rear suspension was a little loose. The front wheel pulls out of line on the road's deeper bulldust and sand sections. When I rode back from the Bowen River Hotel on my first trip, I bottomed out a few times on some of the causeways. An upgraded suspension was needed, so I replaced the standard springs with Cogent dynamic springs and hydraulic dampers and fitted a Moab high-performance shock absorber on the back with a heavy-duty rear spring.

By the time I finished, I had spent over four thousand dollars, but the level of performance is chalk and cheese compared to the standard setup. Emu is now a bike that would go anywhere which I need for the ride to Cape York. For anybody thinking of getting an adventure bike, it's important to mention that, even though I've spent seventeen thousand dollars on my bike and equipment over the past couple of years, it is still cheaper than the stock price of its nearest competitor.

Its closest competitor would also require some modifications to make the journey I'm undertaking. The story's moral is to make good, informed choices about what you need on a bike; understand this will change as you become a better and more adventurous rider. My advice is don't sidestep the time it takes to understand what works for you.

Now is the time to complete the upgrades to the bike and begin my planning for the big trip to the top and the corrugated red dust roads that lie ahead.

Chapter 3
Back to the Beach

"Once the travel bug bites, there is no known antidote, and I know that I shall be happily infected until the end of my life."

– Michael Palin

Riding out on an adventure is becoming second nature to me, but deep inside my psyche is the desire to experience, to explore and to grow as an individual. Even though the beach project is the destination, secretly, it's the journey I'm hoping will help build my resilience. Even though I am anxious about leaving my family, I am buoyed by the opportunity to complete the missing part of my beach challenge.

This day is no different from any other in the tropics during summer. The sun is starting to show itself above the horizon, the air is thick with moisture, and the heat's oppressive.

I am about to wheel Emu out of the garage at six in the morning when my daughter, who very rarely gets up before two in the afternoon, comes through the door. Having spent the night at the boyfriend's house and seeing me dressed in my bike gear, my daughter makes the casual remark, "Where are you going?" I tell her about my unfinished business and how I am going to Sarina to begin my ride up the coast.

About halfway through my explanation, she casually says, "Oh, okay, have a good ride." She goes to her bedroom with a cup of tea and toast, leaving me to it as if I were going to the corner shop. There's nothing like a teenage daughter to marginalise your adventurous spirits!

Emu has been patiently waiting in the garage for the past two weeks, fully kitted out. Once freed from the garage, I pull on the choke and push the starter. He roars into life, and the Yoshimura pipe lets everyone in the neighbourhood know we are ready for action.

The ride to Sarina is about six hours south from where I live in Townsville; I will ride down the Bruce Highway to a friend's place at Brisk Bay, just south of Bowen, before continuing down the highway to Sarina, about fifty kilometres south of Mackay.

My confidence level is much higher than on my first ride; I know the bike better and have developed a high level of confidence on the road. I'm comfortable in the seat, have direction, and am ready for adventure. The moisture in the air is heavy, and the day is predicted to reach thirty-six degrees Celsius; not hot by Australian summer standards, but when combined with ninety-six per cent humidity, it is very uncomfortable to be outside.

I start to sweat from the simple act of handling the bike. I'm grateful to be wearing a new mesh adventure jacket. It has leather around the body armour, but the rest of the jacket is a loose nylon mesh. Once up to speed, the wind cools me, the sweat acting like an air conditioner. Another addition is a Sena Thirty Plus intercom that connects directly to my mobile phone. I can take calls and listen to my Spotify music.

At this time of the morning, the road is busy with school traffic. Mums are trying to ignore screaming kids or organise play dates on the phone. A single motorcycle is not even visible. I ride defensively, trying to avoid blind spots and predict when a car will cross into my lane without warning. It's not a great time to ride, but it's either mums and kids or kangaroos. I'll take my chances with mums and kids over kangaroos anytime. This is because of my ongoing wariness with kangaroos that don't understand that jumping in front of a fast-moving object may harm their health.

The only difference between the mums and kangaroos is that the mums usually drive big steel vehicles, and therefore, the only one who will be injured is me. So, through town, I am hypervigilant. Once on the highway, I feel much safer and can accelerate up to highway speed. The first part of the ride skirts around a mountain with lush rainforests interspersed with cattle-grazing land. It's not long, and I've reached sugar cane fields as far as the eye can see.

I will ride through the towns of Ayr, Home Hill, and Bowen before taking the more picturesque trip to Mackay. This route involves riding through the lava plug field of an ancient land rich in fertile fields and tropical cane farms.

The Bruce Highway from Townsville to the sugar town of Ayr is a fast and easy ride. It's now a dual carriageway most of the time, but where it drops down to two lanes, there are numerous passing opportunities. In contrast, the road from Ayr to Bowen is almost like an old country highway; it's not much fun and is only two lanes, with the occasional passing lane. But the road itself is undulating with poorly maintained edges where deep potholes threaten to make you lose control. Avoiding trucks is the biggest problem for the unsuspecting biker.

It's difficult to get far enough left on the road to avoid truck turbulence, and there are a lot of trucks on this road. It's one of the main arterial roads in the region; the heavy truck traffic churns up the road.

It's still relatively early in the morning, the sun is rising, and it shines directly in my eyes. While it's not time for kangaroos to bounce out from their nighttime feeding, they don't have watches and can decide to jump across the road regardless of the traffic or time of day. As I ride, I keep a lookout for the little bouncing bastards.

Generally, where there is roadkill, more kangaroos will be concealed in the nearby bush. Where there is no road kill, I'm led into a false sense of security.

I ride for one hour to the sugar cane town of Ayr and its sister town of Home Hill. The early morning traffic is sparse. Both towns have sugar-crushing plants. Their massive chimneys spew plumes of white and grey smoke during what's called the "Crush."

But not at the present time. It's summer, which is growing time. The big industrial complexes sit like silent sentinels, watching the bright green fields, waiting until it's time to start crushing the sickly sweet cane again.

This region is rich in history, particularly in the cultivation of sugarcane. The Italian influence is strong in these two towns.

***

Many Italian immigrants came to Australia in the early twentieth century to work in the sugar cane industry after the slave labour of islanders was banned. It's a strange fact of the time. Still, the islander trade wasn't banned because it was wrong to enslave another race to provide cheap labour.

Australia was moving into a period of its political history known as "The White Australia Policy." The Policy was a prominent feature of its federation process in 1901, and was a way of getting rid of the hard-working Chinese and Islander labourers.

***

Let's face it, we don't want hard-working people here; it spoils the ambience of the place. It makes it too hard to be a "laid-back Aussie" if everybody around you is working their tits off. I'm not sure how the hard-working Italians managed to stay, but extensive burial cribs highlight their presence at the Ayr cemetery.

These monolithic cribs show a strong family connection and the degree of their success in the industry and region. As a community, they were highly successful, earning a substantial income from sugar cane, but ultimately worked themselves to death. It would take over a hundred years until they, too, became laid-back Australians.

***

Only ten kilometres south of Ayr is another town called Home Hill. A steel arch bridge joins the two communities in an uneasy peace. When I worked across this region as a TAFE director, there was always competition for resources between the two communities.

***

Home Hill was the first settlement in the region, and the area came under the land lease of the Inkerman Downs Cattle Station, first established in 1864 and named in honour of the battle of Inkerman during the Crimean War, one year after the settlement of Bowen.

As usual, the desire to graze cattle overrode common sense; the property was plagued by ticks, probably due to its low-lying and swampy ground. It was eventually bought by the Government and split up into smaller lots.

As you pass Mount Inkerman on the way out of Home Hill; there's a lookout worth visiting if you want a bird's eye view of the region. The township of Home Hill came into being in 1915 on a dry patch of land near the Burdekin River as a support community for the soon-to-be-opened-up cattle plots.

The name came from "Home Ridge", also called "Home Hill," the British central position during the Battle of Inkerman. I'm always amazed at how heroic war becomes after the initial slaughter quickly fades from memory.

The Battle of Inkerman was as poorly conceived and coordinated as the disastrous charge of the Light Brigade. Yet we see references to it all over the world, including Mount Inkerman in North Queensland, only ten years after the horrendous bloodbath.

***

When I cross the Burdekin Bridge and enter Home Hill, the heat is punishing, pounding down and up. It combines the reflective heat from the tar road with the 80% humidity and thirty-five degrees Celsius air temperature, not to mention my lack of riding fitness. As expected, the ride is beginning to get tiring. I will take a break soon.

***

The Burdekin Bridge is an example of a Steel Arch Road Rail Bridge, with its main engineering structure above the roadway. It is similar to the style used on the Sydney Harbour Bridge. The original bridge was built in 1899, but because it was constructed on the riverbed, it flooded during the wet season, making the main roadway impassable after rain. Building the new steel bridge commenced in 1947 but was not completed until 1957 due to difficulties obtaining steel after the Second World War.

As you ride south over the bridge, the remains of the old Inkerman Bridge can be seen to the left.

***

The ride from Home Hill to Bowen takes about an hour and twenty minutes and passes through the small agricultural communities of Gumlu and Guthalungra. I pull up at the rest area at Guthalungra, a free camping site often full of grey nomads and campervans. The occasional tent is tucked away next to one of the picnic tables.

You can buy fuel and something to eat at the Guthalungra petrol station. I pull up and get my Jetboil out to make a coffee; it's an opportunity to take off my jacket and try to cool down. Having a hot coffee and cooling down is a contradiction, so I drink some cold water before returning to my bike for the final leg to Bowen.

It's a dry, hot road full of worn patches and potholes. Following intense lobbying from the communities, the State Government has been shamed into adding a few passing lanes to this notoriously harmful section of the Bruce Highway.

Truck traffic is heavy on this stretch of road, and I am constantly being blown around. As previously mentioned, I try to ride as far to the left as I can without riding off the road to avoid the pressure wave of the trucks. It's such a narrow road that I'm not always successful.

Chapter 4
Bowen - The Beginning of North Queensland

As I ride down the Highway, I see the turn-off to Abbot Point Coal Terminal on my left and the towering summits of three prominent peaks: Mount Abbot, 3461 ft; Mount Mackenzie, 2024 ft; and Mount Aberdeen, 2904 ft to my right.

When you approach Bowen, you notice an abundance of tomato and mango plantations;. Other crops are also grown in the area. But Bowen is mainly associated with tomatoes and mangos. So famous is Bowen for growing mangos that one variety is called the "Bowen Mango"

Actually, the mango's name is "Kensington Pride," but as it was developed in Bowen, the local growers latched onto the name and used it to promote its unique variety; I'm sure that must have pissed off Mr Pride. It is estimated that tomatoes alone account for an approximately three-hundred-million-dollar industry. It is equivalent to the entire sugar cane industry in the Burdekin region. Bowen played a significant part in the development of North Queensland.

***

The New South Wales government in the 1850s offered a prize of two thousand pounds to any ship captain who could find a deep-water harbour.

Bowen was discovered by Captain Sinclair in 1858 when he was sailing close to shore looking for a port north of Rockhampton. Unfortunately, by the time Captain Sinclair arrived back in Brisbane to claim his prize, the province of Queensland had been declared, and the new Queensland administration wasn't keen to pay for this information. Eventually, Bowen was settled and gazetted in 1861 by Sinclair from the sea and Dalrymple from the land.

Both parties reached the site simultaneously, but there remains a difference *of opinion among the remaining members of the two families regarding who arrived first. Bowen is still the only natural deep-water port in North Queensland.*

It's protected from the dominant South-Easterly wind and the North Westerlies, and became the centre of trade in North Queensland. With gold discovered in Ravenswood and the cattle industry growing, Bowen became prosperous and the centre for further exploration.

***

To explore Bowen, turn left after the Don River Bridge at the Queens Beach sign and follow the road past the football grounds and the high school on the left. The streets in Bowen are unusually wide, a design feature that dates back to when Bowen was picked as the capital of North Queensland. The fact that Townsville eventually became the capital is an interesting story in its own right.

Arguably, Bowen has the best beaches in Queensland, with fringing coral reefs and excellent snorkelling opportunities. It has medical centres, a hospital, restaurants and coffee shops galore, an old movie theatre and numerous pubs. While I would have liked to ride around the beaches and enjoy the salt air, it's getting late, and I told my friends I would be at their place before nightfall.

I spend the night with my friends at their beach house in Brisk Bay; we drink too much red wine and reminisce about past adventures.

The sun rises over the sea, creating a perfect diffusion of colours in the sky, from orange to pink and then purple, followed by a deep, dark blue where the sun's rays have yet to enlighten the heavens. I wake early and brew myself a coffee, trying not to disturb my mates. I start preparing for the next leg of my journey south. It's not long before I hit the road and make my way to Sarina along the Bruce Highway. The route is pretty straightforward, passing through Proserpine and then Mackay. Finally, to my destination, after which I will work my way back up the coast to visit some of the beaches I bypassed on my previous trip when I turned inland to go to the Bowen River Hotel.

I'm looking forward to seeing what I missed along this small but significant part of the North Queensland coast. It's a short detour before I start on my big ride up to the tip of Australia.

Chapter 5
Sarina to Townsville

I leave my mate's place at Brisk Bay early and ride the Bruce Highway through several smaller towns, including Proserpine and Bloomsbury; I take the bypass around Mackay but will ride through Mackay on my return trip.

Sugar cane plantations dominate the area from Sarina to Townsville. Sarina is a sugar town with a giant crushing mill at its southern end. I fill up with fuel at one of the many petrol stations and look around for a place to grab a bite. A sign outside the sugar mill and tourist centre says "Sugar Shack Café." So I park Emu between two giant vans and walk into the shop.

The shop is full of sugar products, from boiled sweets to butterscotch schnapps, chocolate bars, and lollies. I feel like I'm in the fairy tale 'Hansel and Gretel,' my blood sugar is rising just standing there. I have images about getting diabetes, or that I'm about to be put in an oven by some ugly-looking witch.

When I order a coffee with one sugar, I get a strange disapproving look from the barista's face, or am I imagining it? The toasted sandwiches look good, so I order one, settle at a table near a fan, and watch groups of people going on a tour of the schnapps-making plant. I'm not sure if I would do that tour; I haven't seen anyone come out yet, and smoke is rising from a nearby chimney.

After recovering from the heat and humidity in the cool cafe, it's time to get back on Emu and start making my way up the coast. I still haven't seen anyone come out of the schnapps-making plant. I ride back through town, turn right at the roundabout, and head once again through plantations of sugar cane towards the beach.

I arrive at Sarina Beach just after lunch. While it's a beautiful beach with shops and motels, I'm beginning to see similarities in all the beaches: gorgeous golden sand and small crashing waves. The surf lifesaving club is tucked neatly into the dunes.

I walk up and down the beach, but I'm not inspired to stay here, and within a few minutes, I'm back on Emu. I ride in and out of small beach communities; it's the same beach, only different town names.

Emu is purring at around two thousand revs per minute as I ride the coastal road back to the highway. A slight sea breeze blows through my mesh jacket, which cools me off as I wind around beach headlands and small hills. The water is a beautiful, crystal-blue colour, and the view, combined with the slight sea breeze, makes riding a motorcycle such a pleasurable experience.

Eventually, I end up back on the main highway and come across a large roundabout. I can go to Mackay or take the second exit to the Dalrymple Bay and Hay Point Coal terminals. There's a viewing platform up on the hill above the Dalrymple Bay Terminal, so I take the time to ride the winding rural road back towards the coast.

The view over the terminal is spectacular. There are masses of coal stockpiles, each stockpile surrounded by concrete walls. At any one time, over 125,000 tonnes of coal are sitting on the ground waiting to be loaded into the bellies of bulk carriers, some of which can be over 180,000 tonnes.

These giant ships take one of Australia's main exports to hundreds of markets overseas. Meanwhile, trains bring in five thousand tonnes every fifteen minutes.

Giant machines called stacker-reclaimers manage these stockpiles, and they would be ideal props in a War of the Worlds movie. They are substantial lumbering steel structures, each costing upwards of forty million dollars; their sole purpose is to pump the coal from the trains onto the stockpile.

When ready, they pick up the coal with their giant digging wheels and send it to other big machines called ship loaders that pump the coal into the hatches of the bulk freighters. I was told once that, during the coal boom of 2010, eighty-six ships were sitting at anchor in the deep-sea channel waiting to be loaded. Further south, great plumes of water are spraying over the Hay Point stockpiles in the near-futile attempt to reduce the coal dust being picked up by the winds.

It's the middle of the day, and I still have to ride back through Mackay before finding a place to camp for the night. Mackay is a sugar city that has thrived as a support hub for both the sugar industry and the various mining operations in the Bowen Basin.

Like any other regional city, Mackay is a bustling hub of activity; as I ride into it, I'm quickly reminded of its role in the mining industry, with giant factory sheds everywhere and massive 80-tonne coal-loading trucks, dozers, diggers, and fleets of cars. There are hydraulic repair shops and engineering manufacturing businesses everywhere. Further into town is a whole street of motels and pubs, and temporary accommodation for those on business.

Besides the humidity and heat, my first impression of Mackay is that it has a Mediterranean feel. Many buildings are designed in either Spanish Mission style or Art Deco. This is because Mackay was blown down in 1918 and rebuilt in the style of the day. The city sits on the banks of the Pioneer River. I wrote about this river in my first book, 'Gun Fights, Ghosts and Goannas,' and even though I was only twenty kilometres from the river mouth, I had to ride another eight thousand kilometres to reach this destination.

The land that makes up Mackay is the traditional land of the Yuwilbara Aboriginal tribal groups. Europeans arrived in 1860 and set up a small settlement on the banks of the Pioneer River. This township grew into what is now the city of Mackay. It was initially discovered by an explorer and pastoralist named John Mackay who drove cattle over the Yungella Range and into what was to become the Pioneer Valley. Shortly afterwards, the area was opened up to sugar cane farming.

Like the Gold Coast, Mackay has many great beaches. These beaches continue the sandy ribbons that start at Dalrymple Bay and move north. My next destination is Cape Hillsborough National Park, which is about twenty kilometres north of Mackay.

I know I've mentioned this before, but I hate riding through cities. I have to be on the lookout for drivers who fail to see me and change lanes unexpectedly. I try to stay out of their blind spots so they have the best chance of avoiding me, or at least I have the best chance of avoiding them.

It's a relief to get out of the main traffic area and back on the highway north. The topology changes; this area has a volcanic past, and small lava plugs are everywhere. About 20 minutes north is a turn-off with a sign indicating Cape Hillsborough. I take this turn and ride out back towards the beach.

It's a pleasure to ride the small country road, with green fields, large eucalypt trees and the emergence of tropical rainforests.

Between me and the beach is a prominent basalt escarpment that rises suddenly from the green cane fields and orange volcanic soil. It's a great feeling winding up this range with its dark vines hanging over the road. It's cooler than being on the coastal plains. The Cape Hillsborough sign is prominently displayed at the beginning of the national park.

Unlike most national parks I have visited, this one is more like a botanical garden; perched on the escarpment, the lawns are mowed, the toilets clean. The barbeque plates are glimmering in the sun like only highly-polished stainless steel can. There are signs everywhere saying 'No Camping,' and 'Stingers Inhabit these waters. ' I'm unsure if the reason for not camping is the stingers; I suspect these are two different warning signs. If not, we're in a dangerous place.

There is an obligatory crocodile warning sign. Have you ever wondered why they are written in German and English?

Undoubtedly, crocodiles aren't bilingual. It's only a theory, but I reckon crocodiles must have developed a taste for German tourists in the past. Or maybe Germans ignore the signs more than others and tend to get eaten regularly?

At the end of the road is a car park, a caravan park and an access ramp to the beach. It is excellent that the access ramp (made of super-hard rubber) goes down to the beach. I only question the ramp's angle and what happens once the wheelchair gets to the end, especially at the speed generated by the steeply inclined ramp.

I know it's not right, but I couldn't help sniggering at the thought of the poor, disabled person flying through the air over the sand and straight into the mouth of a waiting crocodile. Then, the echo of "Danke schön" (*thank you very much*) as the crocodile slips back into the water and disappears.

One of the good things about riding a motorcycle is that finding a shaded park is often straightforward. As luck would have it, I parked next to an old camper van. Judging by the stickers and set-up, this couple has travelled a lot. Not your usual backpacker's vehicle, this one is a work of functional art.

The man is wearing an old, khaki-coloured, tattered bush hat with holes and worn edges. He's dressed in a Hawaiian shirt with camo shorts and sports a grey goatee. His hair is tied back in a ponytail. Meanwhile, his partner is in a simple summer dress, her grey hair tied in two ponytails, with a faded pink bandana wrapped around her head; both are in their 60s.

They tell me how they had changed their lives after bringing up a family and paying off a mortgage. One day they woke up and decided they didn't need all the shit they had accumulated. They sold all the stuff, except the house, which they rented out and took to the road, which was eight years ago. Every day is an adventure, and every day, they meet someone who lives life to the fullest. Today, they met me.

We shared a chai where the water came from a complicated green plastic storage system sitting on the roof of their van and boiled in a blackened and dented aluminium billy seated on a tiny methylated spirit burner; my time with this couple was magical as they regaled me with their travels around Australia.

Listening to them, I am reminded that time is precious and should be spent on having experiences, not accumulating assets. Because at the end of the day, everything you need can be carried on your bike or, in their case, in their van.

The bay is beautiful, with a wide horseshoe shape about ten kilometres long and backed by tall rainforest trees, with a small headland at each end. If you have ever seen a tourist advertisement of a kangaroo being fed by tourists on the beach at sunset, this beach is where that iconic photo was taken.

Having been to many of the beaches in Queensland, I find this is one of the best so far. I make a mental note to come here camping for a few days. If you are travelling this route on a bike, consider stopping here to experience one of the most tranquil places on the coast of Queensland.

My time here is too short. I wander along the beach from the headland in the south to the headland in the north. Making my way up the ramp is hard yakka; I almost die of heat exhaustion due to the steepness of the climb. I return to Emu, who is sitting patiently under the shade of a rainforest tree. I'm sure if he had been human, he would be sitting with a cocktail in one hand, his straw tattered hat pulled over his eyes, swinging in the breeze on a hammock. After saying goodbye to my new friends, I head off into the western sunset.

Chapter 6
Free Beach Camping

The ride down the escarpment is refreshing as the wind pervades my mesh jacket and cools the sweat on my body. A coastal road winds in and out of small beach communities, taking me past Ball and Haliday Bay before depositing me in the town of Seaforth. It is one of those older beach communities that have been permanently established as a holiday destination, unlike the small fishing communities with their amateurly built fishing shanties built by local farmers and claiming crown land as their own.

Traditional buildings like the swimming pool and an old Art Deco ambulance station herald a different time and culture from the past-paced consumer life of resorts and organised tours that we call holidays today. The parks feature giant trees throughout, and the parkland itself was thoughtfully designed when community parks were an essential part of the beach scene.

Seaforth is another magical spot with long beaches and a large, well-maintained stinger net. Stinger nets are a quintessential feature of North Queensland; if well maintained, they help keep the bigger box jellyfish and, in some cases, the smaller Irukandji jellyfish separated from swimmers.

Swimming in north Queensland differs from swimming on any southern beach. Stingers can kill, but generally only cause excruciating agony for about 24 hours; this is not an understatement. I have seen people in the hospital wailing in pain 24 hours after being stung.

Antivenoms are now available, but the initial medical treatment is to pour vinegar all over the sting site to prevent further poisoning and immediately call 000 for an ambulance. The solution to this jellyfish threat is wearing a stinger suit, a thin layer of Lycra that stops the jellyfish's tentacles from contacting the skin. A stinger suit is an interesting bit of kit. For beautifully shaped women, it stirs the imagination; for chubby old men with beer bellies, not so much. Of course, these suits don't protect you from tiger sharks or crocodiles, so it pays to get advice from locals before swimming in the sea of North Queensland.

A fantastic caravan park at the town's northern end sits behind the dunes. I wander around the park, but it's my goal to find free camping wherever possible, and I know of one such place nearby.

It's getting late, and I need to find the anticipated free camping site for the night. My overnight destination is a small park at St Helens Beach. I punched St Helens Beach into my GPS, and instantly, I'm given an inland route that would take me directly there via Western Australia and the Hume Highway, a mere 12,000 kilometres. I decide this might be slightly out of my way, so I follow the Mount Ossa Seaforth Road and then change to the Mount Pelican Road.

St Helens Beach is a collection of rocks and mangrove trees. The bay is shallow, and the beach is a thin strip of opaque yellow sand that barely cover the rocks. Just back from the beach is a small grassed area and a toilet facility with a couple of picnic tables.

Several expensive off-road caravans are parked to the side and behind the toilet block. They have been there a while, as the camp looked well set up with a fire pit and bins of empty beer cans and champagne bottles. There are no campers in sight.

When I first started "wild camping", I was always nervous; I was anxious about whether I should stay or continue to a safer site. It's easy to make up all the possible dangerous events that may occur any night when you're not camping in a well-maintained caravan park. After all, mass murderers are behind every tree, watching for signs of weakness and waiting for you to start snoring.

Undoubtedly, bad people and miscreant youth float around from time to time. But it's my experience that the biggest fear is in our heads. Provided you're sensible and do what you need to protect yourself, wild camping is fun and will save you a lot of dollars. My mother was a grey nomad who never paid for accommodation while travelling. As a solo traveller in her 60s, she never had any problems.

But it's a very similar planning process to what I covered in my first book about riding out into the desert. If you don't take precautions and prepare yourself for any eventuality, you restrict the number of options available if you encounter problems. I always look around the site before deciding to stay. I ask myself, 'Are there other campers around, and do they look genuine? Is there graffiti? Where can I hide out of the way? Does the area feel safe? How can I get away if things go wrong?'

The St Helens free camping spot is well maintained, with security lights, picnic tables, and clean barbeques. The grass is mowed, and there is a picnic table near the walkway to the toilet block under the shade of a leafy green tree that wouldn't drop a branch on me during the night. It's a perfect place to camp. The sun has slipped behind the trees to the west of me, lighting up the beach in a soft orange glow.

I pick up my camera and wander to the beach. It's a perfect time for photography, so I use it wisely to capture the long mud flats and small mangrove trees growing in the intercostal zone. The golden orange light reflects off the small rock pools of water left by the receding tide. It's almost like a stairway out to sea. Even though it's the middle of the summer season, the wind from the ocean gives me a slight chill. I go back to my camp and begin the preparation for my evening meal.

It's not a complicated process: boil some water in my Jetboil stove, cut the top of my dehydrated spaghetti bolognese pre-packaged meal, pour hot water, seal the bag and wait five minutes—instant gourmet meal for one. As I finish digging out the last spaghetti, I hear the dull rumble of a four-wheel drive in low gear coming up the beach. Its headlights appear like some man-made monster from a James Bond film and it forces its way through the bush toward the camping ground. My neighbours have returned.

A click and hiss of beer cans being opened, the popping of champagne corks and the clanking of glasses; let the party begin! I tuck myself into my tent, and before long, I am woken by the slamming of car doors. Checking my watch, it's five in the morning. I have been asleep for about eight hours, a record for me. Peering out of the tent, I can see several work utes with blokes standing around talking.

No sooner had they arrived than they're gone. It was too early to hit the road, so I got up to make a coffee and wander down to the beach to watch and photograph the sunrise. It's a magnificent time of day. I watch the sky turn from inky blue to orange again. Eventually, the sun peeks over the horizon, and I shoot some awesome sunrise photos.

Watching the sky change, I feel content with the world. I do the mental arithmetic on the cost of my neighbour's week-long fishing trip and how they hadn't caught a single fish. It goes like this: one hundred and sixty thousand dollars for the four-wheel drive vehicles to travel to the fishing spot, one hundred and eighty thousand dollars for caravans, ten thousand dollars for fuel, food and travel expenses and two thousand dollars for alcohol, a total of three hundred and fifty-two thousand dollars. I divided this by two hundred dollars, the average price of a Coral Trout meal for four people at a top restaurant.

That means my camping party, rather than getting hot and sweaty and disappointed at not catching fish, could go to a top restaurant at least one thousand seven hundred sixty times, that's every night for five years. The expedition isn't about the fishing, although that is the object that motivates the travel; it must be about something else.

As I sit and watch the sunrise, I have the strong impression that they are on the same journey as me, spending time in nature, being mindful, and letting the hectic pace of life wash away like the waves crashing on the beach and the subsequent receding tide.

I ride a motorcycle, and they flick a fishing line, but the result is the same (unless they actually catch a fish). Many people travel or purchase items to experience the outdoors; some of these items are costly. It occurs to me that in the end, they want a little excitement and the perception of freedom. The sad part is they have to work for forty-eight weeks a year to pay for everything. I could be wrong, of course; they might just be bad fishermen like me. Unlike me, they might have a lot of money and don't know what to do with it all.

I finish the dregs of my coffee and take a few last photos of the sunrise. I want to return to the road and head towards Airlie Beach in the Whitsundays. Afterwards, I will ride back to Townsville before beginning the next stage of my journey up the coast.

It's early, and many residents of the small fishing villages I pass are still asleep; I hope Emu's load exhaust doesn't wake them. Even if it did, they would be looking for a Harley, not a simple single-cylinder KLR650.

The cane fields look softer in the morning light. I'm far more relaxed than I would be thundering up the motorway. Maybe it's a good night's sleep or the freshness of a new day, but the ride is exciting. I'm rolling into the next corner, accelerating and shifting my weight from side to side.

This is the fun of riding; some people like going fast and racing. I want to cruise, listening to the engine roar as I accelerate out of the corner, rev-matching as I drop down a gear into the corner, leaning over, then straightening up as I come across the next bend.

There's a T-intersection up ahead; turn left, and it's back to Mackay. Turn right, and I ride into Proserpine ten minutes later. I'm ripped back to the busy, hectic pace of life as I turn right. Before I even realise it, I'm slowing down and drifting into yet another sugar cane town dominated by its vast smoke stack.

Today, I am visiting the highly popular tourist town of Airlie Beach. Once a mud track to the resort islands of Hamilton, Hayman, Long, and Day Dream, this town has come into its own, mainly due to its giant lagoon and bathing area. It is billed as the gateway to the Whitsunday Islands and is North Queensland's answer to Byron Bay in New South Wales.

Sugar cane is everywhere. Once described to me as giant grass. I feel like a tiny ant weaving my way between lush green stems in a giant's manicured garden. Cannonvale is located at the end of the Cannon Valley and Airlie Beach, just over a small ridge.

Chapter 7
Kokomo in North Queensland

The Whitsunday Islands are a group of islands best described as tropical paradises. The island groups were originally the home of the Ngaro tribal people and had been for the past ten thousand years after the melting of the last mini-ice age. The first island to be named by Europeans was spotted by Sir Joseph Banks on board the HMS Endeavour during Cook's traverse of the east coast of what was to become Australia in 1770. It was named Pentecost after the Christian festival of the Pentecost.

The Endeavour sailed through the island chain during the "Whitsun" on the seventh Sunday after Easter. It was named the Whitsundays as a result. Cook noted the spectacular white sandy beaches and the alluring colour of the ocean. He, therefore, called the entire island chain the Cumberland Islands and the passage they would sail as the Whitsunday Passage. The Cumberland Islands comprise the Sir James Smith group, the Linderman group and the famous Whitsunday group.

It's only a twenty-minute ride through tropical cane fields and small volcanic lava plugs left over from volcanos that died thirty thousand years ago. I ride through the busy township of Cannonvale, with its modern houses and shopping centres. Suddenly it's there in technicolour!

I see a spectacular ocean view, a marina full of expensive yachts and several sailing boats moored further out in a small bay. Riding over a headland, I am presented with more breathtaking scenery of the township of Airlie Beach and the beautiful azure waters of the Whitsunday Island group.

Airlie Beach started as a gateway town to Shute Harbour. Big boats take holidaymakers to upmarket resort islands like Hamilton and Hayman Islands or smaller resorts like Daydream and Long Island. It is also a place to book tours to the reef for snorkelling and SCUBA diving. Over the past forty years, the town has reformed into a tourist mecca in its own right, with high-end shops, restaurants, cafes, tattoo parlours, and pubs.

It's also a backpacker destination with plentiful work on offer in bars and restaurants on the islands. One of the town's main features is the Airlie Lagoon; this giant swimming pool is my destination this morning. I've been looking forward to taking a swim for some time.

About halfway down the main street is a left turn into a big car parking facility; as it's mid-week, I have no problem finding a place to park Emu. I fish through my panniers to find my clothing and locate my shorts and small travel towel. Although there is no reason to be concerned about security issues, I make sure Emu is parked in the open so that I can glance at him occasionally. I put on his brake lock and alarm just in case.

The Airlie Lagoon is a spectacular swimming pool that stretches almost half the length of the main street. It consists of several shallow areas for kids and deeper spaces over two metres deep for adults. A bridge divides the lagoon; it's a favourite place to dive down and cool off. Around the sides are barbecue areas, showers and numerous toilet blocks. I go to one of the toilet and shower blocks to get changed.

Every day it is a haven for backpackers who lie half-naked during the day and work or party at night.

The lagoon is the central meeting place for backpackers and families, and it put the town on the map when it was opened in 2001. The beach at Airlie is small, and the surrounding seascape has a mud base; stingers plague the area during the summer, so the lagoon is the only safe swimming place. It has become a central meeting place for many young men and women who lie half-naked, sunning themselves on the small hill that divides the lagoon from the ocean.

There is something special about swimming; the water washes away all the positively charged ions, leaving us feeling alive and relaxed.

Swimming around the lagoon and diving deep under the bridge is cool and refreshing. It's such a soothing experience that I float around for over an hour under the watchful eyes of lifeguards who I'm sure were thinking "How the hell are we going to get this whale back in the ocean?". The reality of getting home to Townsville today overcomes my desire to float in the crystal clear waters of this stunning human-made waterway for the rest of the day.

Back on the road, I take a shortcut out of Cannonvale that has me riding through yet more cane fields. I'm starting to feel hungry, and I know of a small beach with a pub about twenty minutes from the main road. Dingo Beach is as close to the mythical paradise of Kokomo in the Tom Cruise and Brian Brown film

"Cocktails" as you can get.

It is worth the ride to the peninsula where the Gloucester Passage divides the mainland from Gloucester Island. There are two main townships here, Hideaway Bay and Dingo Beach. You can stop at the caravan park at Hideaway Bay, but I'm heading for the pub on the beach at Dingo Beach.

Dingo Beach is a small township with a general store, a volunteer fire brigade, and a pub with some unit accommodation. It also has a small boat ramp with a narrow channel leading towards the Gloucester Passage. The boating channel can be seen at low tide, and many returning boats are beached in the channel waiting until the tide comes in, at which point they can be winched onto waiting trailers on the beach.

I pull up at the hotel and park Emu facing out at the beach's edge; the water is glassed out, not even a ripple is breaking the surface, and the tide is starting to come in. A small red trimaran is moored to a line and anchored on the beach. It looks more like a native sailing boat than a modern ocean-going yacht. But it is perfect for the environment it is sitting in.

I get this feeling of being on a tropical island miles from civilisation. If I could undo the anchor and sail away, I would; it's almost perfect. Along the beach, there are barbeque plates, a toilet block and some play equipment for kids.

There's an old stinger enclosure further up the beach. I hear the Beach Boys Song "Kokomo" in my mind and start swaying to the music. I realise the bar lady is watching me, so I explain what is happening in my mind. She laughs, 'Don't worry,' she says, 'you're not the only one.' We laugh together about it and discuss Dingo Beach and adventure travel.

She is about sixty years old, but you would hardly notice. She is your typical experienced bar lady, with a great big smile and large breasts revealed by ample cleavage, a short skirt and a tanned body. She probably knows every local by their first name and is as much of an attraction to this idyllic place as the beach is.

I order lunch and a soft drink. It would be great to kick back here for a few beers and listen to live music. The feelings I have about this place bring back memories of Fisherman's Wharf all those years ago, when I felt that life offered endless possibilities. Then, I remember earlier visions of a dream to live on a tropical island with a hammock strung between two coconut trees and a half-naked, buxom blonde waitress serving me cocktails.

The song "Sitting at the Dock of the Bay" interrupts the Beach Boys' theme song currently playing in my mind. I could live here, but I'd need to get a trimaran. It's a place I will return to, but for now, I enjoy a steak burger, chips, and a glass of lemonade.

After lunch, I sit on the picnic table beside Emu with the red trimaran floating just off the beach. What is it about this place that seems to resonate with my soul? I'm at peace here, far away from the hustle and bustle of Airlie Beach, the constant heat and ugliness of riding a hot, radiant highway, but most of all, I'm far away from the commercialism and tyranny of modern life.

In my adventure around Queensland, I have travelled three-quarters of the way from Coolangatta to Cooktown and visited almost every beach; few resonate with my soul like this one.

I think about one of my favourite writers, Ian Fleming, who created James Bond. He owned an estate in Jamaica called ""Golden Eye" which is where he wrote his novels. From what I have seen, the environment was similar to Dingo Beach. He had a private beach at Orcasbessa Bay on the northern coast of Jamaica. Like many writers, Fleming understood the importance of place for his creative work and as a means to fuel his inspiration.

So far on my journey, I have realised that freedom of the mind is a crucial part of positive mental health. I'm starting to form the view that individuals need to find a place that inspires them and provides them with the solitude to meditate on possible futures.

"My brief immersion in the laid-back vibe of Dingo Beach has opened my mind to the importance of place as part of the creative process. As mentioned earlier, my creative place is the hammock outside my bedroom. Is place a missing link in my creativity or an essential part in my recovery from a lifetime of sleep, eat,work,eat and sleep again cycle?

My insights this afternoon at Dingo Beach tie in with what I've discovered so far on my journey: that freedom of the mind is a crucial part of positive mental health. Creative individuals must find a place that inspires them and provides solitude to meditate on possible futures."

It's time to leave this place and make my way to Townsville. I put on my jacket, helmet, and gloves and push the starter. Emu jumps into life. This is only the second time I have had a revelation about my life on this journey, for creatives like me, place is critical to positive mental health. This is something I need to explore further. For now, I'm feeling free as I imagine the type of place I would like to create to help with my future writing and creativity.

As I ride back towards the cane fields, I feel the back wheel wash slightly on a corner, something doesn't feel right. I should have stopped to check out the back tyre, but instead, I ignored it. About halfway along the access road from

Dingo Beach, Emu begins to wobble; it's the telltale sign of a flat tyre.

I have never changed a tyre on my KLR before, so I found some flat ground near a property that sells homegrown vegetables. Luckily, there is a milk crate at the front of the property covering the water mains. I ask the farmer if I could use it to rest the bike on. I always carry two spare tubes but have never changed a tyre on a motorcycle. I instantly Googled how to do it, and the exact video popped up on YouTube.

The whole episode takes about 30 minutes. I reflect on my thoughts before this adventure commenced; a couple of years ago, I thought changing a tyre was a major mechanical event. Today, it's a minor annoyance that comes with being an adventure rider. The more problems I face, the more resilient I become.

I put Emu back together, ensuring all the bearing seals are in the right places and the tension on the chain is correct. I check the evenness of the axial nuts to ensure the chain runs true, and test the bike before reloading all my gear. Then I go looking for the farmer to thank him for the opportunity to work in his front yard.

The farmer gives me a towel and soap to wash the grease and oil off my hands before showing me around his small farm. He has chickens, ducks, and various vegetables growing on what appears to be half an acre of land. He and his wife make a small living from the produce store out front and supplement that with the fish he catches, eggs from the chickens, and the occasional duck sacrifice. They get their milk mainly from the goats that wander around the back part of the property.

They live a very sustainable lifestyle. They have a great market garden, eat fresh produce, catch fish, and make money selling the excess. If this lifestyle became too stressful, they could go to Dingo Beach and chill for the day or launch their boat and catch more fish for their freezer.

His wife makes a cup of chai for us all, and I sit with them for a while, talking about their lifestyle and my travels. They are a fantastic couple in their sixties, and there's an atmosphere of contentment as we share stories and talk about their lifestyle. I could live like this, although I would struggle to kill the ducks, I'm a bird fan and would have given each of them a name and a unique personality, it would be like killing a family member. I'd have to name them after some of my extended family.

Chapter 8
The Funniest Toilet in Queensland

I have one more stop before getting back to Townsville. About five kilometres past Mount Inkerman, a small sign says, "Wanjunga Beach." When I lived in Bowen and would take my son to soccer in Ayr, I passed this sign weekly. I always intended to go and have a look, but never seemed to have the time.

I'm on my bike, and I can go where I like, so today is the day I decided to go out to Wanjunga. I wasn't expecting a beach. I don't know what I expected, except a run-down fishing community with cobbled together corrugated iron shacks, stray dogs, snotty-nosed children and duelling banjos. The ride out to Wanjunga is more interesting than I thought it would be; for a start, most of the road is gravel, which is a welcome relief. The gravel is interspersed with concrete causeways that criss-cross a wetland.

The bird life in the wetland is immense, and I didn't expect so much in an area hidden from the main road. I hoped to see the occasional crocodile, but the water wasn't deep enough. When I was closer to the community, I could see houses in the background and several tracks leading to the beach. I choose one and ride up the deep sand until I find a place to park Emu. From there, I walk onto the beach.

The beach is long and flat, ideal for driving your four-wheel drive or launching your boat. I'm conscious of time, so I leave the beach to look around the town before my final journey home to Townsville. Not long past the beach track, I come across a caravan park; it's called the "Funny Dunny Caravan Park."

I pull up momentarily to take in the sign; I'll stop here on the way back. It's such an interesting name. Just past the caravan park, the road becomes tar as it rises steeply to the first house in the community. I couldn't get the sound of duelling banjos out of my mind. It occurs to me that there is something strange about this community. It is perched on the edge of a small bluff that leads down onto the beach. There is a mix of old and new housing; although the majority is old, it resembles any other beach community along the Queensland coast.

However, unlike some communities I've been to, this one seems closed off and insulated. I can't see much activity besides the occasional dog barking and people peering out of their windows. The town has no amenities, not even a picnic table or a toilet block. It would be the first community I have visited without these basic facilities. I decide to take a look at what makes the dunny so funny back at the caravan park.

With a name like "Funny Dunny Park," there has to be a story, so I ride into the park, passing an unusual toilet perched on a concrete block. My first impression is that everything is normal with the park, like any other I had been to on my adventures. There are large, flat sandy campsites and a path through the beach scrub to the long, expansive beachfront. A few grey nomads peer out of their vans at me.

I must admit that Emu is not the quietest bike. With his Yoshimura pipe, thumping single 650 piston, and all-black appearance, he sounds like he means business. At the time, I am wearing my black jeans, black mesh, and leather jacket, so I suppose I fit the image perfectly. There are some angry looks as I ride past a couple of vans, clearly disturbing someone's mid-afternoon sleep. Or maybe they think I'm the scout for a much larger "Hell's Angels" confluence.

I hit the kill switch to appease the caravaners and looked around the site. This old dude wanders up to me and starts asking questions about the bike and where I came from. It turns out he's the park's caretaker; his name is Jim, and he lives in his caravan with his best mate "Digit."

Jim is a resourceful dude who not only looks after the park but also sells hardware and other essential caravanning products like duct tape, fuses, matches, lighters, and anything you might run out of. After all, it's a long drive to the nearest supermarket.

For those unfamiliar with the great Aussie colloquialism, "Dunny" means toilet. Remember I said I was surprised Wanjunga didn't have a toilet block? Well, the council thought this was a problem as well. So, they called the town together to ask where they thought the toilet should be placed. Nobody in the community wanted the toilet anywhere near the town.

They were concerned it might attract the wrong sort of people, so they decided to locate it about five hundred metres away from the community. Jim regales in the story of how the Funny Dunny name came to pass. The toilet was built at the time on a platform to prevent flooding during the wet season. When the council decided to allocate some land for a camping ground, they chose the toilet site rather than dealing with the locals again.

While the toilet had survived for about eight years, when the campground was built around it, tourists from all over Australia came to stay and used it (not just to use the toilet, of course, that would be strange!). Then, one day, a grey nomad couple from Melbourne arrived.

The Melbourne lady in her gold and pearl necklace and dressed for the Melbourne Cup was convinced a peeping tom had crawled under the toilet and watched while she did her thing. So confident was she that this incident took place that she contacted the police and the council. According to Jim, her actual words were, "That Funny Dunny at Wanjunga is dangerous and attracts deviants."

The council did not want to attract more deviants, especially those from Melbourne, so it decided to pull down the offending dunny and build a more robust, modern version. Hence, the name and the unusual outhouse that stands there today.

I could have listened to Jim's stories all day; he is typical of some fantastic characters you meet when riding around Australia. Unfortunately, it is time to move on again. I ride out across the wetland and back onto the Bruce Highway.

The rest of the journey is straight up the highway. I ride up the small driveway to my house as the sun is setting. I am home, but only for a short time. I intend to finish the tropical ride up the coast and explore the Daintree rainforest before planning my journey to the tip.

My unfinished business has been completed, and the gap in my best beach research has been filled. The next stage of my motorcycle adventure through the tropics of Queensland is about to begin.

Chapter 9
German-Speaking Crocodiles Again

After a couple of days back in Townsville, I am ready to continue the next part of my journey up the tropical coast of Queensland. I intend to ride through Cairns and Port Douglas, then through the oldest rainforest in the world, over the Bloomfield Track to Cooktown, before turning around and riding the Mulligan Highway back to Atherton and home to Townsville. This will be a total distance of over three thousand kilometres, most on the highway, but I'm planning an enjoyable off-road experience through the Daintree Rainforest.

Before leaving Townsville, I ride to the local beaches to ensure the validity of my beach research. It's early when I leave home, so I ride through town; it's quiet, apart from those annoying men and women in Lycra riding push bikes. Have you ever wondered why they are called push bikes? I've never seen anyone pushing them. On a motorcycle, I'm not challenged by them, but in a car, they piss me off. Not all of them, only the ones who ride two and three across a bike lane. Making it impossible to get past them without changing lanes, as if one lane specifically dedicated to unregistered bikes is not enough. I'm trying to channel my inner peace on this beautiful summer's day.

I see a group of them riding in formation up ahead. It's time for some vengeance. It reminds me of those dogs that wait silently in the back of utes to bark at you just at the right time as they pass by, scaring the shit out of you, and then you see them smirking and wagging their tails. I back off the throttle as I approach the group; as the traffic light changes, I drop a gear and twist the throttle. Emu's deep, throaty engine shatters the peace, and the vibration sends the riders wobbling through the lights. I'm sure Emu would have a similar smile on his face (if he has one).

Townsville has some fantastic beachside facilities, centred around "The Strand" and "Pallarenda." The Strand is a five-kilometre beachside strip of walking tracks and parkland that overlooks the Port of Townsville and Magnetic Island. The road is an assortment of restaurants, hotels and accommodations.

At the southern end is ANZAC Park and Tobruk swimming pool; at the northern end is the Rock Pool and the Jezzine Barracks, a throwback to World War Two when gun emplacements and ammunition storage were all over the city. Townsville is a garrison town and a key military asset in Australia.

The park has been part of Townsville's history since 1910 and was initially known as Strand Park; the name was officially changed to ANZAC Park in 1934. Over the years, cyclones have damaged the waterfront and washed away parts of the beachfrontage. After Cyclone Sid in 1998, the whole foreshore was redeveloped into what we see today.

The beaches are coves between small rocky headlands, spreading along the length of the strip. The water is deceptive: At times, it reflects the crystal-clear azure waters of the coral sea, and at other times, when the wind is pumping and the current is running, it's a grey wash with white caps.

The Townsville Rock Pool is a saltwater swimming enclosure. Some rock pools get flushed out with the tidal movements. The Strand Rock Pool has its water pumped and filtered to reduce the possibility of marine stingers being sucked into the enclosure.

It was time to continue up the Hume Bruce Highway, so I put on my riding gear and weaved through the beachside streets and arterial roads until I was once again heading north towards the sugar cane centre of Ingham. There, I intended to ride to one of the longest trestles in the southern hemisphere. The trestle is 5.76 kilometres long and provides access to large bulk freighters. I plan to sit and have lunch while I marvel at Hinchinbrook Island and the equally spectacular Hinchinbrook Passage.

To reach my lunch destination, I have to ride through Ingham. The vegetation clearly shows that I have crossed an imaginary line delineating Townsville and Bowen's dry tropics from the rest of North Queensland. The topology changes constantly as I continue riding.

***

The same European guy who first mapped Bowen also chartered Ingham. George Dalrymple on an expedition to a cattle station called 'Valley of Lagoons' in 1864 on an expedition to the Valley of Lagoons Station, recorded details of the area. But it wasn't until 1871 that the town was officially gazetted and named

Ingham. Conflict with the local Aboriginal peoples occurred throughout the late 1870s until the native police were disbanded in the region. It seems clear that the recruitment of Aboriginal people from different tribal groups outside of the area did not improve communication with local tribal groups in fact it probably added to the hostilities. A lot has been written about the role the native police played in the colonisation and control of Indigenous peoples.

As I ride through Queensland and find sites of interest, it is well documented that the native police conducted some of the worst atrocities under the supervision of the English. It is nowadays viewed as a failure of the colonial governments to recognise the intertribal hatred and long-time feuds that existed between different tribal groups. These feuds were exacerbated by allowing one group to have guns, which enabled them to wreak vengeance on the others.

By this time, the sugar industry was thriving, and its need for cheap (slave) labour grew. The use of South Sea Islanders swelled the population. It's reported that up to seventeen point five per cent of the slave population (blackbirding) died as a result of injuries or disease. A royal commission into blackbirding outlawed the practice in 1886. However, it continued in North Queensland until 1901, when some of the first legislation enacted by the new Commonwealth of Australia made it illegal.

Many South Sea Islanders and Chinese were sent home after the enforcement of this legislation in what was to be called the "White Australia Policy" However, some managed to evade deportation and remained behind. The South Sea Islanders were the unsung heroes of the cane industry; without their work and sacrifice, there probably wouldn't have been a cane industry.

Many of those families still live in the area. Ingham is also a centre for several Italian families that immigrated to the region. A large community of Italian descent hold an Italian Festival every year in the town.

***

The ride to Lucinda is again through acres of cane fields and past several smoke-billowing sugar-crushing plants. Lucinda is the gateway to Hinchinbrook Island National Park; it's also the main distribution point for refined sugar from the mills in the region. I know of Lucinda from my SCUBA diving expeditions to the Pelorus and Orpheus tropical islands in the Greater Palm Island group. Coral reefs surround these islands, and they are some of the best and most easily accessible dive sites I have explored on the Barrier Reef.

I'm no longer in the dry, oppressive heat that typifies the dry tropics. Instead, I'm in the wet, stifling heat of the wet tropics. Whichever way you look at it, it's hot. Somehow, the damp, oppressive heat seems kinder to me while I'm riding but less so when I'm camping. The mesh jacket I purchased for the trip allows me to sweat and for the wind to cool me as I ride, like an inbuilt air conditioner.

I return to Emu, and we head north once more; as I ride north, and cross the Burnett River. I saw a YouTube video a couple of years ago of a stormy night when a car came across a three-metre saltwater crocodile on this bridge. The sight of the bridge brings back thoughts of crocodiles everywhere. I reflect on how easy it is to become complacent about them in North Queensland. They are in almost every waterhole, and their numbers are increasing.

I think it's too late to brush up on my German. I know two German phrases, "Ich liebe dich", which I believe means "I love you", and "ein Bier bitter", which means "One Beer Please". I'm led to believe that both are essential phrases when picking up a big-titted German barmaid at the Oktoberfest, but completely useless when communicating with a bilingual crocodile that has latched onto your leg. I should avoid waterholes and rivers in North Queensland until I improve my German.

It doesn't take long until I'm riding over the Cardwell Range. I must drop Emu down a gear for the steep, twisting corners. At the top of the range is an excellent lookout. You can see Hinchinbrook Island and the famous Hinchinbrook Passage from it.

The blue water, green mangrove forests that grow to the edge of the passage and the towering monolith of Hinchinbrook Island take my mind away to those war films of the Pacific and conjure images of swaying tropical palms and bikini-clad girls. It's another "WoW" factor, and I smile again.

My previous book discussed WoW factors and Moments as remedies for declining mental health. WoW factors are situations or events that take your breath away and make you feel glad to be alive, while Moments are situations like the instant the sun rises above a glassed-out sea, and you know this moment is unique and memorable.

As I descend the other side of the range, I see a curious site: wire walkways strung up in the deep green canopy of the tropical trees, like some scout jungle course crossing the road. These enclosed suspended walkways are designed to prevent wildlife from becoming roadkill. I can't help wondering how kangaroos climb trees to use them.

I saw another video of one of our local politicians exasperated over a multi-million dollar investment in enclosed wire bridges to help cassowaries cross the road unhindered. Now, for those who don't know much about Cassowaries, they are big, aggressive, flightless birds with massive talons that can tear you apart, a little bit like Emus with bad attitudes. Making them climb trees so they can use the new million dollar bridges is just going to piss them off even more than they already are.

I chuckle to myself every time I see a wildlife bridge in the trees, wondering how many Cassowaries use the bridges. Should we install elevators at each end to assist them in navigating the bridges?

The ride from the top of the range to Cardwell is pleasant; within 20 minutes, I enter the township of Cardwell. Cardwell has cafes, restaurants and motels and is a popular stopping point for travellers to Cairns. It suffered significant damage when Severe Tropical Cyclone Yasi, a category five system, hit it in 2011; a category five cyclone has wind gusts up to 285 kilometres per hour. Yasi tore through the town, ripping off roofs and generating a five-metre storm surge that wiped out the foreshore. I heard from one local that big yachts in the mangroves are still unrecoverable.

The story behind the marina debacle is not widely known; rumour has it that the residents of the upmarket marina units didn't like the unsightly poles, so they all agreed to have the tops cut off. Of course, during the cyclone, the storm surge raised the water level above the poles and the berths, along with the boats, all drifted onto the banks of the marina. Wrecking millions of dollars of boats. Karma is real.

Cardwell is a small town at the top of the Hinchinbrook Passage. Established in 1864, it was a deep-water port for the transportation of livestock and considered one of two possible deep-water ports and capital cities in North Queensland. Bowen was chosen as the favourite due to its more navigable channel and better access to emerging mineral areas. Both Bowen and Cardwell had the only natural deep-water access channels in North Queensland, so in true North Queensland political decision-making, the winner was Townsville. But as a consultation price, Cardwell did eventually get wildlife bridges.

The beachfront is spectacular, but it is known for giant crocodiles that swim out of the Hinchinbrook Passage, sunbathe on the beach, steal fish from the unwary fisher and then return to their deep-water homes, a good place to practice your German.

As I ride further north, the landscape becomes denser which is what I expect of the tropics. I ride through deep, lush green rainforest hills, palm trees and pineapple plantations. I'm approaching another sugar town. Tully is also known as the centre of whitewater rafting in Queensland. The town centre is just off the highway and right next to the billowing smoke stake of the sugar-crushing plant.

It is a significant support centre for the cane growers and the sugar mill and has the record for the highest seasonal rainfall in Australia. A giant fibreglass gumboot located at the rest area stands six metres high. It shows how much rain fell in one season to make Tully the wettest town in Australia.

It's getting late, and I'm starting to tire. I don't have far to ride so I take the time to walk around and stretch my legs. There's a well-equipped rest area in town opposite the sugar mill.

Once you leave Tully, it's not long before you come across the southern entrance to Mission Beach. An Aboriginal settlement was set up at what is now Wongaling Beach under the pretext of keeping the Aboriginal people safe from exploitation by Chinese and European farmers.

Interestingly, in the entire colonisation debate in Australia, there is minimal discussion of the role the Chinese played in Australia's history. Probably because so many of them were deported under the White Australia Policy, and their contributions were left to historians to report. I get back on Emu and head east towards the beach community of Mission Beach.

The name Mission Beach is wrongly attributed to this settlement, which is assumed to be a Christian mission like so many others scattered around the country, which were set up to educate Aboriginal children. In this case, it was a settlement to protect Aboriginal people from exploitation by unscrupulous white and Chinese farmers who had taken over the land. It was initially named the "South Mission." A road was built in 1920, which eventually led to the town's establishment in the 1940s.

Chapter 10
Opium, Slavery and Ill-fated Adventurers

I've always been fascinated with the glossy publicity photos of Mission Beach. The palm and coconut trees towering over the golden sand, the blue and turquoise water lapping gently on the shore. It's the image that sticks in my mind alongside the big-titted waitress serving me cocktails in my hammock. As I ride into town, I'm slightly disappointed, sure, on a good day it would look spectacular, but the town itself is little more than a couple of shops, a caravan park and a ranger station.

Mission Beach is the traditional land of the Djiru people. The first Europeans arrived in the area and got along well with the Djiru. In 1870, Europeans started cutting cedar and clearing land for bananas, mangoes, pineapples, and coffee. They employed the local Aboriginal people to help with cultivation.

However, the treatment of the Djiru people was less than ideal; the farmers were used to having cheap labourers and often didn't pay their Aboriginal workers. Conflict broke out between the Aboriginal labourers and the European squatters as a result of this poor treatment. When they did get paid, it was in rum rather than wages.

At the same time, the Chinese had set up market gardens and were paying the local Aboriginal workers with Opium. The government objected to this treatment of the Aboriginal people. To protect the Aboriginal people from the wicked settlers, the Government established the Hull River Aboriginal Settlement. This settlement provided food and shelter to quell the discontent and conflict between the Aboriginal people and Chinese and European settlers.

This settlement became known as the South Mission, even though it wasn't an actual mission like the others set up by the churches. When a cyclone destroyed the settlement, the remaining occupants were sent to the Great Palm Island mission off the coast of Townsville.

***

Mission Beach today is a small tourist community with hotels, shops, restaurants, and laid-back resorts. However, in recent years, it has grown into a residential community. Mission Beach is known as the southernmost habitat of the Southern Cassowary. As you ride into the Mission Beach area, you're confronted with signs warning you of Cassowary crossings and hazards. Interestingly, there are 45 breeding cassowaries in the area and 47 warning signs about cassowaries. While cassowaries aren't common in settled areas (preferring their rainforest habitat), I have seen one walking through a local caravan park; he's a regular and turns up at the same time every day. I'm not sure, but I think he is looking for a bridge to cross the road safely.

I wanted to explore the area, so I rode to Wongaling Beach at the southern end of the community of Mission Beach; it winds around to the Hull River headland. Hull River is just south of the Hull River headland, there is a walking track from Wongaling Beach to the headland. I ride down towards the start of the walking track. There is a historical marker at the beach; I use these markers to gain insight into the history of a place I'm visiting. This time, I was fortunate to find the marker that documents the exact spot where Edmund Kennedy landed to begin his exploration of Cape York.

***

Edmund Kennedy and his party of twelve adventurers landed here in 1848 to begin an exploration and survey of Cape York. This monument exists to recognise that historic landing. I was researching Cape York and came across this group of explorers. I was surprised to learn they started their inland journey from this very beach.

The party got as far as Weymouth Bay on the Cape York Peninsula, some members were struggling, weakened and ill from hacking their way through the rainforests. Eight of the party stayed behind to be picked up on the return journey with the supply ship.

Kennedy and four others continued until one of the four men in Kennedy's group accidentally shot himself. What the fuck? You're miles from anywhere in a hostile country, and you play with guns to the point that you shoot yourself?

Anyway, ignoring the lack of health and safety and general common sense, I'll continue with my story. Kennedy and the Aboriginal guide Jackey Jackey went on, reaching the Swamp River where hostile Aboriginals speared him, and he died from his wounds.

After he buried Kennedy, Jackey Jackey walked on and met up with the supply ship, the 'Arial.' He guided them back to where the other three of the minor party were camped, but they were all dead. Upon return to Weymouth Bay, out of the remaining eight, only Goddard and Carran had survived.

***

I sat looking out from the monument, reflecting on the bravery of these adventurers. History tells us about the ones who made it, but we don't often hear about those who did not succeed.

To ride to Mission Beach from here you go towards Tully until you get to a small shopping centre, then ride north to a T-intersection and turn right towards the beach.

As the clouds build up out to sea, it's becoming humid, and I expect to be rained on for the first time on my motorcycle tour of tropical Queensland. The surrounding vegetation is a tropical rainforest, and I feel like I'm in a special part of the world.

Mission Beach is world-famous as the place where the rainforest meets the Great Barrier Reef. In reality, there are many places where the rainforest meets the Great Barrier Reef. However, the town of Mission Beach has done a great job of marketing itself. When you come into town, I have to admit it's a letdown because it lacks shops or restaurants that live up to its international reputation. It is more like a laid-back village than a sophisticated international destination.

The beach is spectacular; on the right day, it's the absolute picture postcard of Tropical Queensland. I pulled up at the beachside camping ground, which is thirty-five dollars per night and a little expensive for the small exposed position they recommend.

But I had heard about a smaller camping ground at Bingil Bay, about thirty minutes north of the Mission Beach village. Bingil is an Aboriginal name, meaning good camping place, and it's easy to see why. Lust tropical rainforest goes straight onto the beach.

***

Bingil Bay was originally the location of the very same farmers who paid the Aboriginal people in rum. The farm was developed by brothers Frederick, Leonard, Sydney and James Cutten in the 1880s. They grew coffee, mangoes, bananas and other tropical fruits and exported their goods by small boat (the only way to access the bay then). It wasn't until 1921 that a track was put through to a small community called El Arish. In 1930, a road was built. It should be noted that the Chinese got into trouble paying Aboriginal people with Opium.

While it may seem strange to us in the twenty-first century, knowing what we know now about opium, it's worth noting that it was still legal in Australia right up until the Federal government legislated against it in 1910. In many parts of the country, opium was used as a currency, similar to rum during the Rum Rebellion in the early days of the colony. The Government eventually stepped in to protect the Aboriginal people by building the Hull River Settlement and giving them food and clothing.

***

It was getting late, and I was considering several stealth camping sites when I found the small council camping ground at Bingil Bay. Luckily, the grounds caretaker found a small flat spot near a walkway for me. As I set up my tent, down came the rain, so I quickly got Emu and my gear under cover.

The campground was terrific, with views out over the bay. As the moon rose, it cast a golden reflection on the water. There are times when a view will take your breath away; these are cherished Moments. I had stopped at the hotel and purchased a bottle of red wine. As I sat in the vestibule of my tent, drops of rain ran off the side.

The waves crashing on the beach made for a relaxing end to my chaotic day. For dinner, I opened a dehydrated packet of spaghetti bolognese, poured water from my Jet-Boil stove into it, and let it cook for ten minutes. The freeze-dried dinners are much better today than in my early days tramping through the mountains of New Zealand, where a civilised toilet was nowhere to be found.

Chapter 11
Murder and Cannibalism

At the beach, life is different. Time doesn't move from hour to hour but from mood to moment. We live by the currents, plan by the tides, and follow the sun. "

- Sandy Gingras

It rained on and off all night, but inside my tent, I was dry. In the morning, the clouds had cleared, and the rain had washed away the dust suspended in the atmosphere, the same dust that turns the sunset bright orange, a feature more prominent in the dusty outback than the crisp fresh rainforest. I woke to a beautiful clear sunrise, with flat, translucent blue tropical waters and water dripping from the broad-leaf rainforest trees surrounding my campground.

The temperature is in the mid-20s, and all the humidity built up over the past week has crashed into the rainforest. Strolling up the beach, I found a freshwater stream with crystal-clear water. It looked like the water was gently escaping through the rainforest.

I took the opportunity to refresh my sweat-stained tee shirts and shorts. It's far too shallow for crocodiles, so I sat in the ankle-deep water and let it cool my body and repair my soul.

But in case I was wrong, I yelled out "Ich liebe dich" and "ein Bier bitter" to see if I could elicit a response. But nothing answered back. I wanted to stay longer, soaking up the negative ions from the water and marvelling at the beauty and mastery of the rainforest.

These transformative events occur frequently in our lives, but we often fail to take the time to experience them and appreciate their value to our souls. My body and mind are in complete balance with nature.

The Moment is over as fast as it had arrived. I want to imprint this experience into my mind, so I close my eyes before I leave the water and build a visual image of the scene. It's time to leave, so I pack my tent and gear and take the camouflage cover off Emu.

I decide I'd like a photo of Emu and me on the beach looking out to the sea with the rainforest in the background. No problem, I thought; I'll ride out onto the sand. I walk onto the beach first to check the sand's condition. The tide is going out, and the sand is firm.

With the assistance of a local camper, I move Emu onto the beach. After my fellow camper took a few photos, I started the engine and attempted to ride off slowly. At that point, the back wheel drops deep into the sand, leaving Emu buried up to his bash plate.

With the engine screaming and my poor volunteer huffing and puffing, we eventually returned to the camping ground. A reminder to me in real time: a heavily-laden adventure bike is unsuitable for riding down soft sandy beaches.

The road from Bingil Bay to the highway is well-maintained and tar-sealed. It weaves through pastoral land and rainforest and passes several temporary "Cassowaries Crossed Here Recently" signs; had there been bridges here, I'm sure the Cassowarie would have used them.

The rain last night kept the morning cool, ensuring a pleasant ride to the highway.

On the highway, I continue north toward Innisfail. The sugar cane plantations are interspersed with small creeks and rivers, which are surrounded by rainforest sanctuaries.

As I approach Innisfail, the clouds become darker, and I can feel the humidity building yet again. Rain is imminent, and I wonder whether I should stop and put on my wet weather clothing. Too late; no sooner has the thought occurred to me than the heavens open up.

As I'm riding the Bruce Highway, I'm covered in water from the rain and spray from the occasional truck. I should pull over and let the heavy rain subside. Strangely enough, the sign to Kurrimine Beach (Murdering Point) comes into view at that moment. I have passed this sign several times and wondered why it was so named.

It was your typical tropical beach road, surrounded by kilometres of cane fields on both sides. The road to the point is called "Murdering Point Road", a nod to a violent history. While Kurrimine is the Aboriginal name meaning "rising sun," it is initially called "Murdering Point" by Europeans.

In Australia, there is a movement to change all European names to Aboriginal names. In this case, the name change conceals a particularly gruesome discovery and a source of conflict between the local Aboriginal people and European explorers. The beachside town of Murdering Point has now been changed to Kurrimine Beach.

***

We often talk about the slaughter of Aboriginal people by Europeans, but rarely do we talk about the slaughter of Europeans by Aboriginal peoples. Murdering Point was named after one such event; there's no monument to the sailors who died in the line of duty, unlike the many monuments to Aboriginal people killed during those early days. In 1878, Sub-Inspector of the Native Police, Robert Arthur Johnston, was out looking for a small sailing vessel tasked with surveying the reef. It was a cutter similar to the boats kept onboard much larger ocean-going ships.

The cutter was named "Riser", and it had been reported as missing after not reporting back for two weeks. At the beach, Johnston came across some of the papers carried on the 'Riser'. On closer inspection, he located the ghastly remains of the crew inside an Aboriginal sand oven. It appears the cutter had sunk after hitting Kings Reef; all the crew had survived, only to be killed and eaten by the local Aboriginal people.

***

I crossed over a few causeways and found myself in a rainforest valley. The rain had stopped, and I could feel myself drying out. I was dry when I rounded the corner into the Kurrimine Beach community. Kurrimine is the closest coastal community to the reef and would be an excellent place for fishing expeditions. Just don't run into Kings Reef.

After a brief reconnaissance of the community, I am again back on the road heading for the town of Innisfail. On the way, I will detour to check out a small beach town called Ettay Bay. The road is like so many others in this part of the world, lined by sugar cane paddocks, but it wasn't long before it begins to climb into a rainforest. Winding around tight turns and sharp corners, the road is perfect for riding an adventure bike.

As you ride over the hill, the road takes a sharp and steep downward turn towards the beach. The bay is tucked away at the bottom of this steep road. The rainforest hugs the side of the road, casting a deep green glow of filtered light over the landscape; the beach looks like a secluded tropical paradise. It is a small, secluded rainforest oasis. A caravan park at the northern point, a Surf Life Saving Club in the middle and a small cafe wedged between them.

I park opposite the Surf Club at a picnic table looking out at the silent, teal coloured waters of the bay. There is no surf today, the water is glassed out, not even a ripple. The sand is golden with an orange tinge, having come from the volcanic landscape. Ettay Bay is definitely on my top five list of best beaches in Queensland. In front of the Surf Life Saving Club is a large stinger enclosure, picnic shelters and barbeque plates dot the shore front, many of them under the protection of enormous Banyan trees.

It's getting close to lunchtime, and the rain has stopped. I am keen to continue my journey to the northern beaches of Cairns, but before I leave Innisfail, I want to find some lunch.

The rain that had departed me once I went over the hill now rejoins me as I leave Ettay Bay. As I looked around for a place to pull up to get wet weather gear out, I notice my jeans aren't very wet, and there are no raindrops on my mobile phone. The KLR650 has a comprehensive fairing and, as I ride tucked into the bike, the rain is not hitting me in the legs.

My upper body is getting wet, but as I'm wearing a Merino wool tee shirt and a mesh jacket. Rather than being uncomfortable, the rain has a cooling effect, like having a personal air conditioner. I continue riding until I arrived in Innisfail where the rain finally stops and the sun comes out.

Innisfail is a vibrant community about an hour and a half south of Cairns. It supports the sugar industry and is famous for its gigantic banana plantations. The plantations continue for many kilometres out of town. Just when I thought it will be a dry, hot, humid ride out of Innisfail, it's raining again, this time it's a torrential downpour.

I pull up at a takeaway shop and order fish and chips. I sit outside the shop as the rain buckets down. The hot, salty food is comforting. The gutters are overflowing and it is rising against Emu's wheels.

After my quick and very wet lunch in Innisfail, it's a relief to get back on the road and head for Cairns.

Chapter 12
Cairns and a snub to Captain Cook

As I ride closer to the northern tropical city of Cairns, the traffic starts to build and my journey slows. I'm not a fan of city riding, I have to be on guard for cars changing lanes, stopping unexpectedly and doing right turns from the left lane. Let's face it's not a lot of fun riding through choking exhaust from the traffic, which makes you feel sick.

Cairns itself is situated on Trinity Bay and the Trinity Bay inlet. The city was initially known as Trinity, then Battle Camp, and later changed to Cairns. Most of the area around the town is mud flat. Walking around the foreshore, all you see is the long, flat, muddy inlet.

The town is a tourist centre with cafes, restaurants, pubs and cruise boats that take sightseers to the Great Barrier Reef. I like Cairns, but my goal is to get to Cooktown and ride the famous world heritage-listed Daintree Rainforest.

The tide is in; the water looks turbulent. It isn't the beautiful azure waters of the tropics featured in all the glossy tourist magazines. I am surprised by the colour of the water, as I presumed the beaches of Cairns would be as glorious as the ones south of Cairns.

As it's getting late, I'm looking for a safe place to park Emu for the night and a comfortable place to sleep. I don't find any of the motels or accommodation suitable in the city; it requires me to leave Emu exposed, and in a city with a high crime rate, I'm not prepared to do that, so I continue to the northern beaches in the hope of finding a caravan park.

However, these northern beaches are lovely, and again, with the right conditions, they would be exquisite. For those people seeking luxury, there are many expensive-looking resorts on the Esplanade facing the Great Barrier Reef. I chat to a caravan park owner in Clifton Beach; she suggests I stay at the Ellis Beach Camping and Caravan Park.

The park is situated directly on the beach and features some excellent camping grounds. Ellis Beach is one of those places you could easily miss if you're not paying attention. After the congestion of the Northern Beaches and the chaos at the start of the Captain Cook Highway, you suddenly find yourself out of suburbia and cruising over a small hill. As I drop down towards the coast and the famous coastal route to Port Douglas, the terrain turns to forested bushland. This is one of Queensland's most scenic and excellent biker roads.

Before you get to the Ellis Beach Hotel, you find the caravan and camping park tucked into the right side of the hill. If you arrive at the hotel on the left and directly opposite the stinger nets of Ellis Beach, you've gone too far. It is hot, humid, and getting late, and I wanted to explore this place before sunset.

For the first time on this trip, I decide to rent a cabin for the night. The decision isn't difficult; it's late and I'm tired. I enjoyed my shower, air conditioning and the opportunity to have a good night's sleep in a queen-sized bed.

Ellis Beach is one of my favourite beaches in Queensland. It typifies what a tropical beach should be, with palm and coconut trees along the coast and rainforest behind it. It also features a hotel and restaurant nearby.

Unfortunately, the hotel closes early, at four-thirty in the afternoon, just as people (like me!) are rocking up looking for a feed. I'm not sure the young people running the place understand the concept of hospitality. As I walk past later, I can hear the loud music of a private party in the back room.

I settle into my cabin for the night and luxuriate in the air conditioning, the TV, the charging ports, and the dehydrated meal. All in all, it was an awesome day. I found two spectacular beaches for my 'Best Beaches in Queensland' project.

I am kicking back, watching TV, sipping the last of my red wine from the previous night, waiting for my clothes to dry in the laundry, and thinking about tomorrow's journey. I will ride up through the Daintree Rainforest and over to the Lion's Den Hotel and tick off two of my new bucket list items.

There are so many excellent sections of the coast in Australia that you can ride. The ride from Ellis Beach to Port Douglas and the ride through the Daintree Rainforest are two of the most spectacular in Queensland, if not the whole of Australia. I sleep well and wake up as the sun changes the inky blue sky to purple. I want some sunrise photos for my blog, so I make a coffee, grab my camera and walk the short distance to the beach.

The sunrise is spectacular. The sky slowly changes from dark purple to fluorescent pink and then to golden yellow as a small ball of light comes over the horizon. It grows bigger and brighter as it lights up the still waters of the

Great Barrier Reef. This was another "Moment" in my collection of moments and WoW factors. It's an awesome experience to sit on a tropical beach watching the sunrise on a still-cool morning. It occurred to me that my life has been devoid of these moments, and how it's only when you slow down, stop and look around that you truly experience life.

It's hard to feel depressed when you're looking at such a beautiful sunrise. I am finally at the place I wanted to be and am looking forward to the next part of my adventure, beginning with a ferry ride across the Daintree River.

In his book "Why Buddhism is True," Robert Wright explains the importance of being in the moment. At this time, he explains that the thoughts of the past and those of the future do not represent reality or exist. Only the "now" is real; all other thoughts are an illusion.

This is the essence of motorcycle riding. Because it requires us to focus on the "Now" to stay safe and alert, we don't have time to ruminate on past negativity or possible future anxieties, which may never eventuate. Moments like the beautiful sunrise only exist as we watch and marvel at them. Then they are gone, stored in our memory as positive thoughts for the rest of time.

The coastal road winds along the edge of the Coral Sea, with the high rainforest cliffs on the other side marking the start of the Great Dividing Range. With the beginning of the range so close to the beach, there's an overwhelming sense of awe as you ride beneath the mountain's shadow. On the opposite side lie the blue, translucent waters of the Coral Sea and the Great Barrier Reef Lagoon.

The road south is known as the Captain Cook Highway in honour of the legendary sea captain who charted New Zealand and the east coast of Australia. Recently, there has been a push to reject Cook's contribution in Australia because he symbolises a colonising power. The highway's name has recently been changed to the "Great Barrier Reef Way."

Interestingly, Captain Cook was the first European explorer to run into the reef (Literally!). Still, it wasn't until Lieutenant Matthew Flinders circumnavigated and mapped the entire coast of Australia that the reef got close to its current name. Flinders called the reef "The Extensive Barrier Reefs," and for unknown reasons, this was later changed.

It only takes about thirty minutes to ride along the "Great Barrier Reef Way" from Ellis Beach to Port Douglas. But I stopped for about 30 minutes at the McAllister Range lookout, where I took iconic photos of Emu and the twisting road along the waterfront about 100 metres below. I was in no hurry to get to

Port Douglas, and even contemplated returning to Ellis Beach and riding the road again.

Port Douglas is an oasis in North Queensland. It is a picture-perfect town with upmarket restaurants, hotels, resorts, and fashion shops. The main beach is called Four Mile Beach, and it is spectacular.

I find my way down to the beach, park Emu next to a barbeque rotunda and walk out onto the sand. The golden sand kisses the crystal blue water and is rimmed by swaying palm trees. The beach curves slowly and disappears into the forest at the distant southern end. The sea breeze provides enough pressure to cool you off from the humidity.

Unlike the northern beaches of Cairns, the units don't encroach on the sea; there is parkland, barbecue rotundas and walking tracks. If I compare Port Douglas to other Australian resorts, it would have to be the Gold Coast without the traffic and busyness or the early days of Byron Bay without the hippies and backpackers.

As is the case for many other towns in this area, Port Douglas came about due to the discovery of gold during the Palmer River gold rush. It was established in 1871 after James Mulligan discovered payable gold at the Hodgkinson River in Cape York.

At one point, the town had an estimated twelve thousand residents and fourteen hotels. Once the Mulligan Highway was developed, it became a support town for the communities along the highway as far as Herberton. It was also the main export port for gold and tin.

The main road up to the Mulligan Highway joins the town of Mossman, just north of Port Douglas, to Mount Malloy. This road winds up and over the Great Dividing Range in a twisting, climbing zig-zag pattern.

Port Douglas declined after 1933 once the Kuranda Railway from Cairns was built and the town bypassed. However, in 1984, the Cairns International Airport was opened, and during the 1990s, the infamous Christopher Skase built the five-star Sheraton Mirage Resort on the dunes of the famous Four Mile Beach.

Other entrepreneurs arrived, and Port Douglas became a tourism mecca for the rich and famous. In 1996, US President Bill Clinton and First Lady Hillary Clinton stayed in the town, cementing the town's position as an upmarket go-to destination for the rich and famous.

I rode around town looking for a place to stop and make a coffee with my Jet Boil stove. On the town's western side, some parkland is located near the old wharf, overlooking the estuary. There's a great sense of history and colonialism here; the Banjan trees are huge and provide a calm, sheltered spot to take a break from being in the saddle.

Removing my adventure boots felt fantastic as the tropical breeze cools down my feet and the stones below massage them. Two well-dressed, middle-aged women with pearls and gold dripping from their necks and wrists walk by and stare at me with a slight hint of annoyance, or is it disdain? Who cares.

After my second cup of coffee, it's time to travel to the Daintree Rainforest, so I put on my boots, jacket and helmet and ride out of Port Douglas.

Chapter 13
The Daintree: The Oldest Rainforest in the World

My thoughts about Port Douglas seep into my consciousness; it is truly a spectacular and fitting culmination of my ride up the Captain Cook Highway. I can't help thinking how it must have looked to those early explorers seeing this landscape for the first time—images of swaying palms, azure waters and endless golden beaches fringed with deep green rainforests, contrasting the dark, cold, built-up industrial cities of London or Whitby in the 1870s.

I read somewhere that a person was sent to Australia for the term of his natural life for catching one of the King's fish in the Thames River in London. I can't help but chuckle at the irony. Imagine you were fishing in the highly polluted, sewer-infested Thames River and someone sends you on a "free" sailing cruise around the world to Australia with its rivers and oceans teaming with the Barramundi, Mackrel and Coral Trout, its balmy tropical nights, and azure waters. How cruel could life be… poor fellow. The English had a strange sense of justice.

The road towards Mossman is busy as tradies and support workers travel to and from Port Douglas to service the large five-star resorts and hotels, creating a regular stream of cars and utes. Mossman is a typical country town and support centre. It has shopping centres, pubs, mechanical workshops, and motels. It is famous as a gateway to Mossman Gorge, part of the Daintree World Heritage area, and a national park in its own right.

It is worth visiting the national park and walking the bush tracks to enjoy the fresh flowing water of the gorge. Having been there several times over the past twenty years, I'm not inclined to go back again. I must stay focused on my current mission to ride the Daintree Rainforest and the Bloomfield Track.

I continue my ride through the country roads leading to the Daintree rainforest. It's an enjoyable ride; the road twists and rises before dropping and twisting again. I come across a Barramundi farm and a sign telling me to turn right to access the Daintree River Ferry.

The Daintree River comes into view right in front of the ferry office. It's wider than I expected, and is one of the most crocodile-infested waterways in Queensland. I'm not sure 'infested' is the best word to use, as the crocodiles aren't pests unless you are a German tourist, of course. However, the crocodiles might disagree with me about their favourite food source.

So there should be no thought of swimming across the river. For adventure riders on smaller bikes, the Daintree River can be crossed by motorcycle further up the road. It is the first hurdle to riding the infamous Creb Track. Most adventure groups riding the Creb Track take a drone to scout the river for crocodiles before crossing.

The ferry is crucial to the story of the Daintree Rainforest. Building a bridge would have been relatively easy, but public pressure prevented future development. The area north of here is unique in that it involves two world heritage areas: the Great Barrier Reef and the Daintree Rainforest. In the Daintree, life is slower. There is no electricity or other services, and all facilities must be self-sustaining with either solar or diesel generators.

The Daintree is considered the oldest rainforest in the world and is estimated to have survived more than 120 million years. It has sparkling clear creeks, deep green jungle and pristine beaches. The battle between the jungle and the ocean is fought on the sand every day and night as the tide comes and goes. I'm sitting on Emu, and we are at the front of the Daintree Ferry, looking across the waterway to the other side.

In the distance is the beautiful, lush green forest, and the equally spectacular river below the ferry. I reflect on my journey so far. The coast from Coolangatta to the Daintree River is over two thousand kilometres as the crow flies. Emu and I have ventured almost twelve thousand kilometres together all over Queensland. And while I have seen some incredible sights on this journey and met some interesting people, I have been looking forward to this section of the ride more than any other.

Today, I ride the Bloomfield Track, an impossibly steep jungle dirt road at the end of the Daintree Rainforest. I'm a little anxious about the ride. I've driven it in a four-wheel drive, and it was a challenging drive.

I'm looking forward to doing it on a bike. I will end this day at the famous

Lion's Den Hotel before travelling to Cooktown tomorrow.

In 1988, the Daintree Rainforest and its surroundings became the Wet Tropics of Queensland World Heritage Site. This area also includes land south towards Cairns and north to Cape York.

Disembarking, the road winds up Mount Alexander; it is tar-sealed to Cape Tribulation but relatively narrow. As soon as you enter the rainforest, the temperature drops, and you can smell the scent of water, vegetation and moss that grows everywhere in the shade. The forest canopy closes in on you, and the light becomes mottled by the deep green canopy. The experience on a motorcycle is surreal; in a car, you don't get the same connection with nature.

It is not long before you reach the top of the first hill; to your right is the Mount Alexander Lookout. This is the best place to get a bird's eye view of the Daintree River and the wet tropics area south of the river. The lookout is the perfect place for a photo. The rock wall is framed by lush green forest, and below is the snaking Daintree River, far behind the faint outline of The Great Barrier Reef Way.

The ride down Mount Alexander has tight downward winding bends. Water trickles out from the side of the hill and creates small, wet, mossy areas across the road. You could easily slip on these if you are going too fast. There's little time to make course adjustments in the corners before you straighten up and lean into the next corner.

The rainforest is all around you, sinking low; you narrowly miss vines and tree branches. The vines look like hoop snakes waiting to catch unwary riders. The forest gets darker as you move further down the hill; and you can feel the moisture in the air. It is all calmness and you feel a sense of serenity.

The trees are sucking up the radiation from the sun that is so damaging to human physiology. Riding through a rainforest is one of the best motorcycle journeys I've done so far. I come down into a long spiral corner, and on the right, I see a side track; the sign says Daintree Discovery Centre.

I've been here a couple of times with my kids when they were younger. If you want to learn about the rainforest, this is the place to stop; you can also buy a coffee and lunch. The centre has suspended walkways and a large tower that takes you through the different strata in the forest. When you reach the top, you can see the forest below.

The road continues for thirty five kilometres until it reaches the township of Cape Tribulation, at which point it turns into the Bloomfield Track. Along the way, the road runs beside the ocean, with palm and coconut trees leaning out over the sand. An assortment of rainforest trees encroach on the sea, competing with the palms for survival.

Along the road I spot numerous signs for rainforest accommodation and cafes throughout the Daintree. You can visit the homemade ice cream factory with its vast variety of tropical orchards, and they even grow tea here. Small bays separated by crystal creeks are situated up the coast to Cooktown, each of them with its secluded beach.

I pull over at the Thornton Beach Cafe for a cup of coffee, but unfortunately, the cafe is closed. The cafe is on the beach, so I walk onto the beach from the veranda and take some photos; it's a great beach. The water is a beautiful azure colour, calm and inviting.

There was a tragedy here several years ago. Two women were swimming waist-deep when one felt something brush past her leg. She heard her friend call out in panic. The friend was never seen again; it is believed a crocodile took her.

Crocodiles have been seen on these beaches and at the famous Cape Tribulation beach. They are ambush predators and usually don't feed in the sea. However, during breeding season, they have been known to travel up and down the coast in search of mates. As inviting as it looks, it's not a place to go for a swim. Along with the Crocs are the ever-present Box jellyfish and the smaller but more deadly Irukandji.

The road from Thornton Beach hugs the beach, with the occasional small bridge over crystal-clear creeks. It is a spectacular ride, one that every biker should do again and again. Several campgrounds are available on or near the beach, including one at Cape Tribulation called Cape Trib Camping. I was looking for a place to get some food when I came across the Ocean Safari Resort.

This place is targeted at environmental, adventure-conscious backpackers. It serves great burgers and barista coffees. I enjoyed my lunch and felt prepared for the last part of today's journey. I come to the end of the tar-sealed road past the township. From here, it's bush track and wilderness.

Chapter 14
Encounter with a Cassowary

I park Emu at the back of the Cape Tribulation car park and walk in my adventure clothing past all the four-wheel drives and backpacking campervans to the beach. Cape Tribulation Beach is one of the most beautiful beaches in the tropics. The rainforest comes right onto the beach. At the southern end is a thick layer of mangrove, living in the intertidal zone. At the northern end, the beach spreads out in a big horseshoe bay to a distant headland.

The water is a bright, translucent blue, with a patchwork of darker blue sections extending as far as I could see into the bay. These darker patches are small bommies of coral that eventually grow to the surface of the water, indicating small coral reefs. One of those reefs, about fourteen kilometres out, is called Endeavour Reef after it surprised the HMS Endeavour on a calm night in 1770. The ship struck the reef and became stuck.

Many attempts were made to free the ship, but even if freed, a big hole in the side meant the boat would sink if pulled away. A young seaman suggested they sling a sail around the bow of the ship, and once it floated off, the sail would cover the hole. With all hands, including the captain manning the ballast pumps and the makeshift sail fixed in position, the crew were able to pull the ship off the reef and sail up the coast to eventually beach the Endeavour for repairs at the inlet of what was to be known as Cooks Town.

In a contemplative mood, I sit for some time imagining what it must have felt like for Captain Cook, his officers and crew to face the very real prospect of being stranded in a strange and hostile land.

It is time to continue my adventure and ride the Bloomfield Track. After you leave the Cape Tribulation car park, you climb over a hill and descend a potholed dirt road until you come across your first obstacle on this track: a wide creek crossing. Emmagen Creek is usually a shallow crossing, but it can change quickly with rain.

It has a firm rock base, but sometimes cars not equipped for the journey get stuck and churn out big holes, which are traps waiting for the unwary biker. I arrived there just after two four-wheel drive tourist buses had turned up.

I expected the creek crossing to be deserted, but it had become a meeting place for almost fifty Korean backpackers. When they saw me check out the water level, they all lined up on the side to watch and take photos as I rode through (no pressure).

The creek is usually flat with a loose rocky base, but should be crossed with care. I let my feet drag through the water as I bounced across the creek, being ever-vigilant for Mr or Mrs Crocodile. They have been seen in this creek before.

Luckily for me, it wasn't too deep; it would have been embarrassing to drop the bike here. When I make it to the other side, there are wild, appreciative cheers from the watching tourists. I was tempted to yell back, "I'll be back at four for the next crossing; don't forget to book."

I read a story in the Adventure Bike Magazine where the BMW Safari sank over half the BMWs in Emmagen Creek. They left traction control on, and when the bikes hit the rocks, the traction control took over, and the riders dropped their bikes.

I am now riding the Bloomfield Track which winds through some of the steepest parts of the Daintree Rainforest. The track is in relatively good condition for the first couple of kilometres, not as rough as the road to Emmagen Creek. Most people drive to the creek and then turn around, making the road full of potholes. This road is for serious travellers.

Once you get to the Donovan Range, the road starts to climb. It's steep; not only is it steep, but it also has frequent twists and turns. This is not a road you want to ride in the wet; even though the council has laid concrete up the steep sections, you still have to be mindful of any water on the road. Lichen forms on the concrete; if you hit that on the bike, you will slip over or lose traction.

If your bike starts to slide, there's no way of recovering it, and it'll slide down the hill, if not over the side or the track. It had rained last night, but generally, the road is dry; I lined up the wheel tracks and twist the throttle. The KLR 650 has a lot of low-down torque, and I had no problem climbing the steep uphills.

Halfway along the track, I came across Donovan Creek. A strong concrete bridge crossed over the creek, but the entry and exit to the creek were incredibly steep. I stopped in the middle of the bridge, turned my engine off, and removed my helmet and gloves.

It was a good time to let Emu's brakes rest as I took in the tranquillity of the slow-moving river. There were distant sounds of birds I hadn't heard before, and close by, other birds sang out as if to answer them. I listened as more birds joined the chorus. What I thought was a tranquil scene deep in the rainforest was now a symphony of bird song, underscored by the gentle sound of water running over rocks.

It was another "Moment" to charge my soul. I stood there listening and absorbing the sounds of the forest. It was all so seductive, and I wanted to stay longer, but it was getting late, and I had no idea how long this ride would take. So I went through the helmet, gloves, and glasses process, pushed the starter, and Emu fired up.

Off the bridge and on my way again, I rounded the corner and was surprised to see a cassowary and a chick standing on the road. I hadn't seen a sign warning me that cassowaries were crossing in the area, nor had I seen any million-dollar "Cassowary Bridges". Maybe all the cassowaries from down south have come north to escape the signs, unwanted attention and the stress of having to climb trees and cross bridges?

This is a potentially dangerous situation. Cassowaries have killed people before, especially when they are protecting their chicks. The male cassowary incubates the eggs and looks after the chicks for nine months, when they are almost fully grown and can defend themselves. They can be aggressive and have huge, robust talons. I pull over and stop; ordinarily, I would have turned off my engine and watched. But something told me this wasn't a good idea. There was an uneasy tension between us, as the Cassowary held my gaze.

He was about eight metres away, looking directly at me with the chick between us. We faced off for what felt like an hour, but in reality, it was only minutes. I would have taken my camera from my tank bag. It's not every day you see a cassowary in the wild with a chick, but I didn't want to move, and if I had to get away in a hurry, I didn't want my camera bouncing around my neck.

Then he casually turned and strode quietly into the forest; the chick followed. After another minute, I gun the engine and head up the track. As I passed the spot, I looked into the forest but there was no sign of the cassowary or his chick.

The riding is enjoyable, apart from the occasional four-wheel drive ute coming around a corner at redneck speed. And while I would love to take the corners faster, the steep downhill combined with the crazy speed of the local drivers makes me think twice about riding quickly into the corners. I decide that caution and safety are more important than speed and excitement. Even with my cautious approach, the riding was some of the most enjoyable I had experienced on this trip.

The Daintree Rainforest is a spectacular place. When I thought I was coming to the end of the track, there was another turn and another steep dirt hill to climb. This was followed by another steep downhill with another sharp corner and then another concrete section approaching the clouds.

Coming down from the clouds, I am unpleasantly surprised by the departure of Emu's back brake. I was favouring the back brake fairly hard coming into the corners. Pulling too heavily on the front brake would have made the front wheel slide into the corners. This is what made putting a road through the Daintree rainforest so tricky. To do it properly would have required destroying much more of this precious forest.

As I reached the top of the concrete road, I could see the Bloomfield River winding its way around the dense forest landscape below. I am not far from Wugal Wugal, an Aboriginal settlement. This is the end of the Daintree World Heritage Area; from now on, there is only agricultural land. The view from the top of the hill is another picture postcard moment, so I stop to cool down, reflect on my journey through the forest, and take some photos.

I remove my helmet, gloves, glasses, and jacket. It is time to let the back disk brake cool down. Walking around Emu, I check for hydraulic fluid leaks but couldn't find any. The hydraulic fluid has overheated and possibly burnt; I would need to change it at some point to get my back brake working effectively again, but for now and the rest of this trip, I will be content to pump the brakes a bit and use the front brake a little more.

I return to Emu, and we ride down to the Bloomfield River before skirting around the Wujal Wujal community. It's important to check that you don't need a permit to pass over Aboriginal land. You can usually find out from the local and state government websites, or some maps will highlight areas of Aboriginal land. This is not such an issue in Queensland, but in the Northern Territory, you must pay a fee and arrange a permit.

The road from Wajul Wajul is a delightful ride through grazing land and the occasional forested area. It's about forty kilometres from Wajul Wajul to the Lion's Den Hotel, and it takes just under an hour to get there.

Rain has been plentiful this season, so the grass is long and bright green. As it is getting late, the trees are creating the usual zebra patterns on the road, and the grass is potentially hiding kangaroos that would soon be on their nocturnal adventures.

However, I arrive safely without misadventure at about five o'clock. There are no campers in the camping area, and the low dark clouds and high oppressive humidity are threatening rain, so I opt for a cabin and unpack my gear. Afterwards, I head to the bar for a couple of beers and a red wine.

Chapter 15
A Biker's Right of Passage

The Lion's Den is a classic Australian hotel built in 1875 to accommodate travellers to the gold fields and miners from the nearby zinc mine. It is a rite of passage for adventure bikers because it sits at the culmination of the Bloomfield Track and the more complex and notorious Creb Track. For this reason, it is a favourite stopping place for adventure bike tours and is ideally situated for a day's ride from Cairns.

There is some contention as to the origin of the name. One myth is that it came from Daniel, a stowaway who jumped ship at Cooktown and made his way to the tin mines in Helensvale. As he left the mine, another miner commented that Daniel looked like he was entering the Lion's Den (a biblical reference). As a frequent bar customer, the story was told repeatedly until the publican decided to call the hotel the Lion's Den. The other story is that it was named after a pub in England.

The hotel is a corrugated rustic building with a stone floor, rough-cut wood posts, and panels. The bar is your typical remote Queensland hotel, and as with many outback hotels, it has its assortment of ladies' underwear, business cards and naked girl pictures on the wall. The inside of the bar is brimming with artifacts and cultural objects depicting the early days of settlement, including the obligatory young naked female painting above the bar.

Unfortunately, nobody seems to know the identity of the young lady or why she was displayed above the bar. Supposedly, she is one of the most beautiful ladies of her time.

The names of all the people who have visited the hotel have been scribbled all over any spare space on the outside walls and every post or wall panel available. My name would eventually be added to the wall, and several of my 'Digitalswaggie' business cards are strategically placed around the bar. The outside walls are painted to depict the story of the Lion's Den hotel. They tell the story of Daniel. I sat outside on the veranda at the western end of the pub in a place called "Daniel's Dinner."

The veranda is enormous and could easily cater for over 100 people. Rainforest trees poke through the floorboards, and strange-looking orchid-type plants hang from the forks in the trees; I sipped my red wine slowly while devouring a fresh flame-cooked pizza.

I reflect on my day from Ellis Beach, through Port Douglas, across the Daintree Ferry and over the Bloomfield track. Some of the most spectacular scenery in Australia and one of the best adventure riding trails of all time. To top it off, I faced down one of the planet's most aggressive, dangerous birds. In one day, I experienced a lifetime of "Wow" factors and found serenity in a very special "Moment" in the middle of the oldest rainforest in the world.

When I started riding adventure motorcycles, I never dreamed of having days like today. Don't get me wrong, the thought of having an adventurous life drove me on this journey in the first place. But the concept of "WoW" factors hadn't entered my psyche. To explain, if you consider mental health as a pendulum, where everyday life tilts the pendulum to the left. The longer the pendulum stays on the left, the more depressed you become.

When it has remained there so long that you think these feelings are normal, the brain writes these feelings and the associated behaviours into its cognitive structure. This cognitive structure is what creates our behaviours. I believe this is where depression kicks in; life becomes so negative that all hope has left your life and, with it, all your positive energy. It even becomes a massive effort to get out of bed.

The more time I spend contemplating the concept of WoW factors, the more I believe they are what balances the pendulum; the more WoW factors, the more balanced your life becomes. In everyday life, these WoW factors are created by your loving relationships and your children's achievements.

However, the dynamics in relationships change, especially when your children become independent or your relationship evolves into one of convenience, lacking passion and intimacy. At this point, there are no WoW factors in your daily life to balance the pendulum and often no one to talk to about it. In my case, I saw my life continuing as a kind of rat race where there would be minimal reward for my efforts.

Consider the man in a loveless marriage; he was in love at the beginning. The world was beautiful, and he was happy with his partner. Over time, he and his partner had children, a mortgage and a seemingly happy life, but they grew apart. He had a job and a career, and she had a job and a career. She started criticising him for small things. He felt bad and blamed himself; she ignored him and his needs.

He stayed in the marriage for the children, but his self-esteem suffered, and he could only see the darkness, not the light. Now imagine this went on for years and years: no intimacy, no sex, no love, just work. It sounds sad, but it happens to many men and women trapped by obligation in a loveless marriage.

Some men decide life is not worth living, and they commit suicide. It is possibly one of the reasons that suicide rates for men between 45 and 60 are the highest of any age group. Others work through their issues with their partner. Some separate and look to pursue happiness in another relationship. It's a growing trend that men significantly outnumber women in the suicide numbers. They feel their loved ones would be better off without them; that everyone would be better off without them.

I've met people on the road who are so down on themselves that they express themselves in these despairing terms. It's sad because that's not true. Their family would be devastated, and all he had to do was reach out and talk to someone or get out and experience a different life. WoW factors are the light; every time I experience one of them, it takes my breath away, and little by little, the pendulum moves to the right, and the light becomes brighter.

Adventure motorcycle riding does this; it gets the man out, opens the world and provides WoW factors and moments. In some cases, it brings back to the individual a sense of independence and resilience. In the first part of my journey around Queensland, I talked about the meaning of life. In this second road trip, I realise there's more than the freedom of our spirit, important though it is. There is a tranquillity and enlightenment in observing and appreciating our natural environment and meeting other human beings on our journey; it is these experiences that make life fulfilling.

There are a couple of locals in the bar and one young guy travelling around Queensland in his ute, trying to find out-of-the-way waterfalls for drone footage. He has filmed some spectacular scenery. I would have loved to talk with him for longer, but he is off to a beach to camp overnight so he can capture some sunrise footage. After a couple of reds, I head back to my little green worker's cabin for the night.

Chapter 16
An Evil Mountain

The following day, I rise at five and boil my Jetboil stove. After a couple of cups of coffee and breakfast, I'm ready to hit the road. It has rained overnight, only enough to clear the sky of dust but not enough to make the road slippery. Mist hangs over the hills, but the temperature is pleasant. The humidity will rise again as soon as the sun comes up. Before getting to Cooktown, my first stop is the mysterious Black Mountain National Park.

Within minutes of riding, I come across the Mulligan Highway, the main road to Cooktown and a sign indicating the Black Mountain National Park. The Black Mountain is a pile of monolithic-looking rocks that rise approximately 300 metres above sea level and well above the surrounding forest landscape. These rocks are stacked on each other; it looks like a giant has scooped up a load of giant Lego bricks and pushed them into a pile to make a mountain.

They are so dramatically different from the surrounding landscape they look like they could have been placed there intentionally. The local Aboriginal people refer to Black Mountain as "Kalkajaka," which is believed to be a sacred site. They believe it is an evil place and should be avoided.

The legend recounts an ancient battle that took place here between two warring clans. These clans are represented by the black cockatoos from the inland, who are said to have encroached on the hunting grounds of the white cockatoos from the coast.

Many myths surround the Black Mountain. Over the years, people have gone missing while exploring the many passageways between the giant granite boulders. It's claimed that even search parties sent to find the missing explorers have disappeared.

As I stand alone in front of these monolithic structures, I feel a sense of uncertainty and anxiety. I can't wait to get back on Emu and continue my journey.

After a short break to read about the myths and legends from the viewing area, I returned to the road again. It's still early, and the sun hasn't risen above the hills. I want to visit an important landmark and a few fascinating beaches. I'm told a lot of this area is Aboriginal land, but I don't need a permit for where I'm going.

About eight kilometres past Black Mountain, you turn right onto Archer Point Road. The road is well-maintained dirt, and signs proclaim it Aboriginal land. After about one kilometre, it branches off. You should take the left branch. The right branch goes to freehold Aboriginal land, and you can't access the coast from there.

Archer Point is at the northern tip of a large bay that is environmentally significant as a dugong habitat. It has a couple of beaches, free camping areas, and an important lighthouse perched on the headland overlooking the bay.

The bay and headlands are a unique ecosystem. The sheltered bay, steep headlands, and magnificent fringing coral reefs provide a sheltered habitat for dugongs.

The track up to the Archer Point Lighthouse is steep, rutted and twisty. From the beach, it rises sharply and zigzags up to the point. Riding up the track is easy, and I have lots of traction with the adventure tyres. The KLR650 is known for its low-down torque and easy climbing ability.

At the top of the peak, parked next to the lighthouse, is a four-wheel drive ute with a canopy over the tray. I disturbed the older couple sleeping on a mattress in the back under the canopy. They got up when they heard Emu approaching and started boiling a billy. They offered me a cup and we sat on a nearby rock and talked about travelling and the lighthouse. There was a shared camaraderie between the three of us, almost like a fraternity of travellers. I strolled around the lighthouse as they packed up. The view was spectacular, with the mottled sky and the glow of the rising sun behind us; the lighthouse looked older worldly, almost like an old painting. Below was the sheer cliff, and behind us, the steep rolling green hills of grassland.

The light provides a 'Lead light' for sea traffic entering Cooktown and for those that are navigating the narrow passage south to north and central

Queensland ports. It enables ships to navigate between Hope Vale to the north and various reefs to the south. If you're travelling in a vessel, the light will show white if you're in the correct channel, green if you're starboard, or red if you're port to the channel.

After sitting for sometime watching the colours change as the sun rose, I had to ride down, while I hadn't appreciated the steepness and how narrow the road was to the lighthouse, it be came more obvious when I began my journey back down; not only did it seem steeper as gravity was now pulling me down, but I also had less control and relied on both front and back brakes. I could now appreciate the cliffs on the seaward side that I had marvelled at when sipping on a coffee, but now became dangerous obstacles and impediments to my desire to stay alive.

I could only avoid the washouts and potholes by riding a small section of the road about six inches wide close to the cliff's edge and crossing the washouts with my front wheel pointing directly downhill. I couldn't use my back brake as it would have skidded off the edge, and engine braking would have had me going too fast for the corners.

It's a slow, heart-racing descent using a light touch on my front brake. At times like these, I am grateful not to have permanent ABS or traction control.

The Archer Point jetty was established to support the export of tin from Leigh Creek mine, located eight kilometres south near the Lion's Den Hotel. It also supported the movement of supplies inland to the gold diggings of the Archer River gold rush and surrounding cattle stations. Today, its jetty is disused and falling apart, and rusting iron supports stick out from the concrete foundations and rotting wooden pylons.

The ride out from Archer Point didn't seem as long as the ride in. Once on the Mulligan Highway again, it was only a short eight-kilometre ride until I realised my twelve-month quest had almost ended. It was time to get to my final destination.

When I set off from Coolangatta to ride as many accessible beaches as possible, my goal was to get to Cooktown in far North Queensland. Cooktown is one of those towns that has a frontier vibe. It is named after Captain Cook after the HMS Endeavour was beached to make repairs after running aground near Cape Tribulation.

Chapter 17
Cook's Town and the Journey Home

What courage would it have taken to sail around the world with no maps, no hope of rescue if you sank, and hostile people attacking you when you stepped ashore? Did they do this for adventure, money or fame? On 17th June 1770, Captain James Cook of the British Royal Navy and his crew wrestled the wrecked ship HMAS Bark Endeavour into what would become known as the Endeavour River and a small patch of land which would become Cook's Town.

The town wasn't established until 1870 when gold fever hit the Cape York Peninsula and miners poured into the region. It wasn't long before hotels, brothels, and opium dens were established. In 1888, the Sisters of Mercy built a convent in town. The convent is a majestic building that today hosts the Cooktown Museum.

The town is a mixture of the old and the new. Modern hotels sit next to colonial architecture, and run-down shops are next to modern cafes. The Cooktown lighthouse is on the hill overlooking the town and shining out to sea. Captain Cook spent hours here trying to find a channel through the reef to take the Endeavour safely into deeper water. Today, ships are guided through this same channel from the Archer Point lead lights.

The road to the lighthouse is up a short, steep hill that spirals to the top as you ride up. It's steep, and I imagine Captain Cook walking up this hill each day with a group of his marines. He would sit on top with his telescope, surveying the sea. Other members of his crew would sail longboats out under his direction to measure the water depth.

There's a cafe overlooking the town. I park Emu outside and sit in one of the comfortable chairs, looking up the town's main street. It's so hot, I'm sweating, my mind wanders to how the history of Australia is tied to this place.

If Cook had not been such a fantastic navigator and leader of men, and had he given up when the ship was wrecked on the reef and abandoned it, this place may not have existed. Australia would likely have been a different country, and I might not be riding my motorcycle around it.

After coffee, I walk through the Endeavour Park, where a bronze statue of Captain Cook exists. It's fitting to have such a monument in the town that bears his name. Australia would be a different place without this man and his brave crew. Perhaps the Dutch or possibly the Portuguese would have colonised it.

I walk along the river to the mouth. It was somewhere here that they beached the ship to repair its hull. There's so much history here, so much that is uniquely Australian. A land of strong, tough people whose wealth was won by hard work in an unforgiving and hostile environment.

I make a pact to go further north; one day, I will document the ride to Cape York. But for now, I'm content to end my northward journey here. It's hot and humid, and only nine-thirty in the morning, yet I feel drained from the heat. It's the type of heat that seems to radiate from everything: the road, the walls of buildings, and even the grass seem to be radiating heat. It's like being in a giant oven.

It was time to leave as I stood looking up the main street of Cooktown, the temperature was in the high thirties, and the humidity was around ninety per cent. This is summer in the tropics, not a pleasant place to be unless you're a lizard.

While I would have loved to spend more time in this magnificent part of the world, it would be a long day of riding in the heat, so I set out to find a petrol station and make my way home.

I had contemplated riding back past the Lion's Den and up the Bloomfield Track. But since I hadn't ridden the Mulligan Highway before, I thought this might be an interesting diversion, so I would forgo my return ticket on the Daintree Ferry.

After fifty kilometres, I arrived at Lakeland Roadhouse. I didn't need fuel, but stop to take photos of Lakeland Park and the historically-painted toilet block. This is where the Mulligan Highway and Peninsula Development Road (PDR) meet. For those going to Cape York, this is where the adventure starts. I will do this journey soon; it has been on my bucket list for about a year.

The Mulligan Highway swings inland from the coast toward Lake Land National Park before weaving up onto the Great Dividing Range at Mount Malloy. I stop for a break at the Palmer River Roadhouse. In 1873, one of Australia's most significant gold rushes occurred almost precisely where the roadhouse now stands.

It's funny, I feel like getting into the gully below the roadhouse and searching for a nugget of gold. Maybe they missed a bit, or perhaps a rock fell in, revealing a new, previously missed gold vein. This is how gold fever begins; in fact, I can feel a touch of it as I sit eating a burger and washing it down with a can of ginger beer.

In 1872, two brothers from Victoria, William and Frank Hann, were surveying the area. They named the Palmer River after the Queensland Governor who sponsored the exploration. During the expedition, they discovered gold.

A follow-up survey by James Mulligan confirmed the gold's payability, and the gold rush began. It is estimated that more than 100 tons (old imperial measurement) of gold were pulled out of the river during the rush. That's about $8,082,229,259.00 in today's money.

Cooktown became the main port for prospectors and grew substantially. At the same time, an inland track to the Palmer River was being forged, which became the Mulligan Highway.

The rest of the drive along the Mulligan Highway is hot and humid; it takes a toll on me and the bike. I ride faster than usual, averaging one hundred and twenty kilometres per hour; it's times like this that I wish I had a sixth gear. Emu is sitting at about 5,200 rpm, and after 284 kilometres and before the town of Mount Malloy, I feel the engine misfire and start to lose power.

Hunting for the fuel peacock, I twist it sideways to reserve while keeping my eyes on the road; Emu fires into life again and picks up speed. The constant higher revs have used up more fuel than I anticipated.

The rest of my trip home is fairly uneventful, but as big dark clouds build over the range, a thunderstorm was brewing, a big one by the look of it. Camping in the middle of it is not an attractive option.

I ride through Atherton and find a motel for the night, as well as somewhere to park Emu undercover. The motel is situated in a beautiful garden that overlooks the Misty Mountains and descends through rolling hills of green grass. The motel room is spacious, modern, and air-conditioned.

As I secured everything for the night, the heavens opened up for the most earth-shattering storm. Ferocious lightning raged across the sky, thunder boomed, rattling the windows. It was a good choice to stay inside.

I arrived home after almost two weeks on the road, having again taken another step forward in my riding abilities and knowledge of what works and what doesn't in motorcycle touring.

Sitting, enjoying a coffee in the lounge room of our air-conditioned home is slightly surreal. It is a million miles from the solo adventurer's life.

It's almost a year and a half since I began riding adventure motorcycles. I've gone from tenuous wobbles around roundabouts to riding steep dirt tracks and facing off against killer cassowaries. My general dirt riding ability has improved, but not to the point where I consider myself a skilled rider.

However, I am learning that riding an adventure bike and becoming a good rider is more than good technique on the bike. It requires you to read the road and understand the road conditions. It also requires you to be aware of your limitations and not push beyond your skill level.

Sitting in my hammock with my eyes closed later that night, I recall the moments I experienced during my adventure, like sitting in a fresh water creek in the rainforest at Bingle Bay or on Ellis Beach at sunrise; or on the concrete railing of a bridge in the oldest rainforest in the world, listening to the birds sing and the sound of water running over rocks and WoW factors like facing off against giant killer birds. Each moment and WoW factor relived is food for my soul. I'm almost ready for my trip to the Cape.

Trimaran moored at Dingo Beach

Airlie Beach Lagoon

Camping at St Helen's Beach.

The lighthouse at the entrance to Bowen Harbour. One of the best views in North Queensland.

The Funny Dunny at the Wanjunga Beach

Cribs in the Ayre Cemetery show the close family connections of the Europeans who came here to grow sugar cane.

The Sea View Hotel is one of the many hotels along the Strand Park waterfront in Townsville.

Lucinda Sugar terminal, the longest trestle in the Southern Hemisphere.

Ettay Bay Surf Life Saving Club

Giant Gum Boot at Tully showing its record for the highest rainfall in Australia. here to grow sugar cane.

Rainforest Creek, Bingle Bay

Camping on the beach at Bingle Bay

Sunrise Ellis Beach, a definate 'WoW' factor.

Emu looking south along the Captain Cook Highway (Great Barrier Reef Way) towards

Old Storage Shed, Port Douglas. Taking a coffee break.

Emmagen Creek, Daintree Rainforest. Korean Tourists getting back in their tour bus after the brave adventurer made it across the creek.

Crocodile on the Daintree River. A timely reminder of the dangers that lurk below.

Emu parked on WukuJu Creek bridge, just before my encounter with a Cassowary and the infamous Donovan Range.

The famous Lion's Den Hotel, a right of passage for adventure motorcycle riders.

Black Mountain, a war between the Black and White Cockatoos. A sacred place.

Archer Point Light is still used for navigation by vessels entering and passing Cooktown.

'Cook's Light' on the 'Grassy Hill'. Emu is parked where Captain Cook would have been taking his bearings to map the reef and sail safely out of the Endeavour River in 1770.

Chapter 18
Learning to Ride in the Mud

After returning from Cooktown, I became even more obsessed with the possibility of riding to Cape York; it is now an obsession. However, as with my first adventure, I start doubting my skill levels. Could I ride one of the most dangerous and isolated roads in Australia?

I was reading blog posts from other adventurers about riding it solo. I knew it could be done, but a nagging voice said, "You're not ready for such an adventure. Look at those guys and the bikes they're riding, now look at you and Emu. Do you compare?".

Deep down, I know it's bullshit; Emu is every bit as capable of taking on the "Cape." My hesitation is because I'm not sure about my riding skills, and there will always be some doubt in my mind about whether I can handle it, at least until I get back. One of the important lessons I have learnt over the years is how it's best not to overthink an issue, especially one where the outcome is unknown.

Robert Wright, in his book "Why Buddhism is True," recommends that meditating on keeping your mind in the present moment allows you to disassociate and analyse your thoughts of anxiety. He reasons that the thoughts that tell you you're incapable are seeded in preexisting behavioural patterns. Likewise, an anxious thought is no more real than the dream you might have of the future; both are illusions.

It's a bit like a situation I found myself in when teaching my seventeen-year-old daughter to drive. We were coming on the highway, approaching a narrow bridge over a crocodile-infested river. Coming the other way was a large cattle truck, known in Australia as a road train because of its extra size and length.

My daughter wanted to stop and allow the truck to pass, but I told her to keep going, reminding her that she would often be in this situation on the roads of outback Queensland. She asked me what I would do if I were driving. I told her I would close my eyes and hope for the best.

This is probably not what you should tell your nervous teenage daughter when approaching a giant truck with a combined collision speed of two hundred and twenty kilometres per hour, and you are supposed to be the responsible parent.

But as I told her, once we had passed the truck, "We were in our lane. There was plenty of room; truck drivers are experienced at pulling their rigs straight in these situations. Apart from the truck swerving into our lane, which we had no control over and is unlikely, we were going to pass it comfortably." If it helps to remove the object of your fear from your conscious mind, then by all means, close your eyes. However, I would prefer you keep them open.

I probably should qualify the above statement lest I get arrested by the police for child cruelty. My daughter was a good driver with lots of experience, and I had the utmost confidence in her, but she lacked some confidence in this situation. If I had let her stop, she would not have learnt how to disassociate the fear from the situation.

I have a saying: "If it doesn't kill you, it makes you stronger." If it does kill you, then you can say to yourself, "I told you so," and be happy in the knowledge that you were right all along.

The desire to ride to Cape York is growing stronger, almost to the point of obsession, as is my anxiety about making the journey. I am practising mindfulness and reading extensively about Buddhism and meditation. Whenever I feel overwhelmed by anxiety, I focus on the present and allow the negative thoughts to float into my mind. I metaphorically push them away with my hands.

However, I am all too aware of my limitations as an off-road adventure rider, so I join a Facebook group for the North Queensland Adventure Riders and sign up for several of their rides. Many of the riders in this group are highly experienced and offer expert riding advice.

One particular ride is a three-day expedition to the Gulf of Carpentaria. It is the perfect opportunity to test Emu's new suspension on a real off-road excursion and see how comfortable the sheepskin cover I just bought will be for long rides.

The ride to Einasleigh was more than an adventure rider's rite of passage; it was a test of endurance. The weather forecast was for wet and cold conditions, and my helmet visor fogged up with every breath I exhaled. When I lifted it to wipe the water off, the rain penetrated my eyes like pins and needles. I thought, "This must be what it's like to ride in England on a mild summer day."

The annual Christmas in July event is a nice ride through the Great Dividing Range from the coast and along a well-maintained dirt road to Einasleigh in the Gulf Country.

The event allows adventure riders in North Queensland to come together, catch up with old friends, and meet new ones. However, because of the rain, I estimate only about 28 of the regular 70 riders attended this year.

My journey started in Townsville. I ride over the Great Dividing Range via the Harvey Range crossing and then west to Bluewater Creek. At Bluewater Creek, it starts to rain, and by the time I get to the Greenvale Roadhouse, it's pissing down. So that you know, Pissing Down is an official Australian category for the weather. Used mostly in Victoria where it seems to 'piss down' all the time. It refers to a lot of water in a short period.

This lady at the petrol station asked me if I was going to Einasleigh for the bike meeting. I said I was, and she explained that she was taking the ute as a support vehicle. I would have joined her on the trip, but I was concerned the road would be challenging to ride in the rain.

I had heard of a lot of mud and washouts on the road. Usually, the Einasleigh to Lynd Junction road is a well-maintained dirt track about eighty kilometres long. It joins Einasleigh to the Gregory Development Road and heads into what's called the Gulf Country. This area leads to the Gulf of Carpentaria, which is a short distance down the road. In Australian terms, it is about five hundred kilometres further north. Today, it was more creek than road, with deep mud pits.

An alternative route would take me past the famous Undara lava tubes and a short access road to Einasleigh. I have long wanted to explore this road. It starts at Mount Surprise, which is about fifty kilometres further west than my current position. It would add two hours to my journey.

Mount Surprise has an interesting and varied history; originally, it was a support centre for mining activities. This area, including Einasleigh, is known for gold and copper, and prospectors still wander about picking up nuggets; later, it became a centre for cattle grazing.

During World War II, it was a relay station for the telegraph line from Charters Towers and a remote communication repeater. It would transmit communications of Japanese fleet movements in the Pacific Ocean to the southern command centres.

I pull into Mount Surprise; the rain has stopped. I'm meeting the Townsville and Cairns adventure riders who have also decided the road is too wet and are taking the shortcut. We commence our ride as a group, but it isn't long before the BMW and KTM riders are out in front, racing each other. As usual, I'm at the back on one hundred and five kilometres per hour for most of the twenty-five kilometres of tar-sealed road before the dirt road turnoff.

The "short cut" is a wide dirt road with corrugations and long, deep-cambered corners, perfect for adventure riders. Throughout the trip, I encounter pockets of muddy track that are getting deeper and longer the further we move into the valley.

This was my first time riding mud tracks with my new suspension. Even though the suspension was significantly better than the stock gear, my anxiety increases as the mud becomes deeper and mud trenches become longer.

Had it been my old suspension, it would have dived when entering the mud, causing the front tyre to corkscrew. There would have been a lot more movement and a lot less direct drive to the rear wheel.

However, with the new set-up, I could average about one hundred kilometres per hour on the flat areas, floating into the corners and accelerating easily. The modifications increase my confidence in Emu's off-road performance. In the mud, I drop down a gear and cruise at about fifty or sixty kilometres per hour. The fear of getting thrown off in the mud is almost paralysing.

I catch up with two riders, Nardeen from Einsaleigh and Dave from Cairns. Dave is on a GS1200. Nardeen, who is new to adventure riding, is on a KTM390. Dave is providing coaching. He leads her through the mud and points out the best line. I follow, doing precisely what they do, and it's not long before my riding improves and my confidence starts to build. It becomes an enjoyable experience, so I intentionally power-slid out of the corners. Emu responds beautifully to my improved technique and effortlessly pulls out of the mud patches like a pro; I can hear him say, 'It's about time we had some fun. '

My anxiety disappears, and eventually, we ride over the bridge into Einsaleigh as a group. It is a fantastic feeling, having conquered one of my biggest fears. But I'm still concerned about how we are going to get home. It looked like rain has set in, and I would have to contend with much more mud on the way out, especially if I go home down the Lynd Junction road.

The view of the Copperfield Gorge from the road bridge is spectacular, with the famous rail bridge in the foreground. This area is known for copper and gold mining, and Einasleigh is established to support the activity. The railway is a significant part of this support network.

It is one of the first private railways established in Queensland in the late 1890s. It was used to transport copper ore from Einasleigh and other small towns to the smelter in Chillagoe, about one hundred and fifty kilometres north east. The railway and smelter have long since been closed down.

Nardeen and the BMW rider ride off to Nardeen's house to join the other adventure riders from Cairns while I make my way to my booked accommodation at the lodge. I am there a day early, but plenty of camping spots are available for an extra night. It is extremely wet and best described by one rider as the Copperfield Waterpark.

I park Emu near the homestead, trying to find some solid ground. Emu sinks into the soil straight away. There is a rock nearby, so I hold on to the handlebars while stretching for the rock which must have looked comical. I place the rock under Emu's stand to stabilise him, take two steps, and sink to my knees in the mud.

Chapter 19
Camping at the Waterpark

The camping spot for adventure riders is six inches deep in water, and more rain is predicted for the next couple of days. The thought of camping with more rain on the way is discomforting. The manager's name is Fran; she has come out to meet me with an umbrella for me.

She's dressed in wet weather clothing and Wellington boots and is one of those typical country women who is not only supremely competent in all things practical, but also friendly and enjoyable to talk with. We chat about the lodge, how it was initially set up to provide accommodation for miners, and how she worked for the mining company.

We slosh through the mud, looking for the best camping site. Eventually, she suggests I pitch my tent in one of the causeways between the little units. This sounds like a much better plan. Then she mentions a room that nobody had booked. If I didn't mind, it didn't have an air conditioner or hot water, but it was mine for half price. How could I resist?

Looking at the drizzle, which has settled in, and then at the comfortable bed in the unit, I find it hard to reconcile the cognitive dissonance between not pitching a tent and the fact I had ridden all this way with my camping gear. It took microseconds to overcome my mental anguish.

After unpacking and spreading my wet gear on every hook and high place and putting Emu's cover over him, I change into some warm clothes and walk to the pub for a beer to catch up with some of the Townsville team, who also arrived early.

The Einasleigh Hotel is the most prominent building in Einasleigh. It is a two-story mansion compared to the other buildings in the town. Built in 1908, it is located on the town's eastern side, directly in front of the Copperfield Gorge; the pub takes centre stage in many activities.

It used to be called the Central Hotel, and it's hard to believe it now, but back then, there were five hotels in the town. The Einasleigh Hotel was the last one standing when the mineral rush died after the Great War. Interestingly, according to Wikipedia, all five hotels were owned by women. I'm not sure what that said about the gender dynamics back then, but I can't help feeling there's a story there somewhere. I clock that away in my mind for another story in the future.

Jamie, Dale, and Dom had come through the Valley of Lagoons from Cardwell and were sitting with a group of other riders who had come down from Mount Surprise shortly before me. The track through the Valley of Lagoons is a steep, undulating dirt road. Typically, it is a pleasant, albeit challenging route. When wet, it would be torturous and only for the best riders. They enjoyed the ride over slippery, near-vertical roads and deep, greasy clay pans.

They are regaling us with the virtues of KTM 890s and sitting drinking beer. Paul, who had ridden his KTM1290 from Mount Isa (about 800 kilometres), sat beside Dom's wife. As it turns out, this was the lady I met at Greenvale who had the sense to drive the four-wheel drive and stay warm and dry.

She politely listened to her husband and co-riders describe their near-death experiences. By now, my wife would have wandered off and probably been looking at the plants in the garden with a glass of white wine in her hand.

Paul is an ex-rally rider and the group's sage guru. There's not much Paul doesn't know about adventure riding, so I sit down with him and quiz him on every riding situation I could think of, even what it's like to ride to the Cape.

It's late in the afternoon, and it's definitely beer o'clock, so I had a beer to wash down the mud that had found its way into my mouth, but I soon found a good bottle of red and had a few glasses before dinner was served.

There wasn't much choice from the menu; it was either battered or crumbed fish and chips. So I chose the fish and chips battered. It's been a long time since I have had fish and chips served in a hotel wrapped in a newspaper. But when in Rome....you know the saying.

It starts to rain heavily, and I feel lucky that I have my wet weather jacket on. At about 9 p.m. I wander back to the lodge, check that Emu's cover is in place and that he's not going to sink into the mud. I jump into bed and quickly fall asleep.

The following day (Saturday) is quiet; I walk around town, taking advantage of some leisure time, capturing photos of the large flocks of screeching galahs. There are some interesting sights in Einasleigh if you look closely. I don't know the back story of the teddy bears at the railway station, but there were about eight hanging or sitting on swings under the Einasleigh Railway sign.

When everyone is awake, I go to Nardeen's place and introduce myself to the Cairns crew who arrive at the same time. They are staying on Nardeen's veranda. After several hours, I return to the lodge and get Emu out of bed.

I ride past the pub and see the Townsville group sitting on the hotel veranda. I make a sharp U-turn and park next to several other adventure bikes; and make my way up the inside staircase. Old pubs have some curious design flaws; either that or people were a couple of feet shorter than they are today.

Walking up the stairs, I hit my head on the second-floor main beam; I duck under it and pull my arms in to squeeze up the stairs. I'm sceptical it would pass any modern building inspection; for some reason, it's only four feet, six inches high.

I start to think about when this pub was built; I wonder if it has any ghosts or if ghost encounters have been recorded. Most old Queensland pubs have ghosts. It's almost mandatory, especially in a mining town. Why not Einasleigh?

One of the guys staying in the hotel last night mentions there is a hatch door in his room. He said, "I checked it was closed and locked before going to bed. I even tried to open it, but it looked as if it hadn't opened for years, and they had painted over the latch." He was adamant the hatch would not budge. "This morning it was unlocked, and the hatch door was wide open."

After this incident is related, Dale and Dom have their own spooky tale to tell. During the night, they heard footsteps going backward and forward along the veranda. This may have been another guest in a room on the other side of the veranda. The problem is the old boards flex and creak when you walk across the veranda. At no time did any of them hear a creaking noise.

You know that feeling you get when you see the light go on in people's eyes, and they look around in amazement at what they have discovered? Add sheer terror to that look. That is the feeling we all have sitting there; the hairs on my neck stood up. Is there a ghost at the Einasleigh Hotel? You be the judge, but I'm thankful to be staying at the water park tonight.

I'm not saying the mood on the veranda became subdued or the thought of ghosts in the rooms terrifying, but everyone agreed it was a great idea to explore the gorge, even though it's raining heavily again.

Queensland has seven well-known tourist gorges, from Lawn Hill to Carnarvon. Copperfield Gorge is rated as one of the easiest to access—once you get to Einasleigh. It is spectacular in many ways and was formed during the volcanic activity that shaped the landscape in this region, including the famous

Undara Lava Tubes.

This gorge is carved out of basalt and has an almost moon-like landscape. When it is wet, an incredible waterfall cascades into the gorge at the southern end, filling it with blue-green water. There is a big sandy beach is at the other end of the gorge

After my morning walk and exploration of Copperfield Gorge, I return to the lodge for lunch. It's not long before I hear the telltale exhaust note from the bikes of more adventure riders pulling into the Copperfield Waterpark.

First to arrive was Bob on his trusty modified KLR650, closely followed by Barry on his Triumph Tiger, Steve on his Versey 300, Jeff on his CB500X, and Dean on his DR650. Everyone went about making introductions to new people and exchanging greetings with old friends.

The camp kitchen becomes the place to be for swags and makeshift camping arrangements. Fran encourages this arrangement, even suggesting that tents could be set up on the causeways between the units.

It's a constant battle to find sticks or rocks to put under the side stands to prevent the bikes from falling into the mud. Eventually, camping gear is set up, units are claimed, and bikes put away for the night as the rain starts to fall in earnest again.

For most of the late afternoon, we sit around talking about bikes, bike adventures, bike accidents, and bike modifications. Soon, it's time to go to the pub for the much-anticipated barbeque. We catch up with other bikers and regale each other with road conditions, bike conditions, bike accidents, bike adventures, and the possibility of separating North Queensland from the rest of Australia in a bloodless political coup d'état.

It's an excellent opportunity to meet socially with adventure riders you rarely are able to catch up with in person during the year. We all ride at different times and don't always agree on what makes a suitable riding destination.

Dinner consists of steak, sausages, rissoles, and at least three salads. To participate, you purchase a paper plate for $25 at the bar and go outside to fill it. You could go back as many times as you liked, or at least until the paper plate fell apart.

Chapter 20
Riding Mud

The next day, we all pack up, eagerly anticipating the final stage of our adventure bike weekend. Packing the bikes and ensuring everything is in its rightful place took the usual time, after which we make our way to Fran's veranda for the best ten-dollar breakfast in Queensland. I make sure to clean the mud off my riding boots before walking across the veranda.

Fran and her friend provide the usual country hospitality and big breakfast, which includes sausage, eggs, bacon, mushrooms, onions, tomatoes and gallons of freshly squeezed orange juice; all for ten dollars ahead, with proceeds going to the Royal Flying Doctor Service (RFDS), a life line for rural people. After breakfast, I join the others, packing our bikes and riding down to the pub to get the obligatory bike photo outside the hotel.

Unfortunately, not all the bikes are there, only those at the lodge and the hotel. It rained all night; Narrelle mentioned she recorded eighty millimetres of rain overnight. This much rain is concerning. Some of the guys who had ridden from the Lynd Roadhouse yesterday hesitated to ride back that way with more water on the already sodden, potholed road.

The shortcut is cut off just outside of town; there are two options. Take an extended trip further west and back onto the highway, which will add another four hours to the trip. Or, ride straight down the mud road to the Lynd Junction. The Valley of the Lagoon survivors lead the conversation, and a communal decision is made to ride the Lynd Junction Road. After all, it was an adventure ride....right?

Jaime and Dale will continue from Lynd Junction and out through the Valley of Lagoons, back to Paluma, and then on to Townsville. The rest of the group agree to ride to the Lynd Junction and down the highway back through the Harvey Range road.

We know it's inevitable that we are going to encounter patches of mud. But as soon as we turn right onto Lynd Junction Road, we hit it—not only in patches we could avoid, but also mud right across the road. I am riding in the middle of the group. Determined to ride faster than feels comfortable, I am trusting Emu to perform as needed.

However, I'm not ready for that much mud, and not so soon into the return trip. It takes me by surprise, and I instinctively slow down. Jeff and Steve fly past me, waking me up to my promise to speed up and ride aggressively.

By accelerating and standing on the pegs, I allowed Emu to show me how good an investment my "Moab" shock, heavy-duty springs and shock dampers were. He was performing brilliantly, it's I who needs to step up.

But the water is not my biggest concern. The mud is about eight inches deep, and there are giant potholes you could lose a car in that the council had 'fixed' earlier. But there's a big problem: the council has filled the potholes with dirt rather than road base, and the dirt has turned into deep, slushy mud.

We are riding down a mud-soaked road, trying to differentiate the giant muddy pits from the surface mud that covers the entire road. All I could see was two kilometres of flat, muddy road ahead. The thought of corkscrewing off at speed sent panic waves through my body.

Dean is staying at the back to ensure everybody's safety; he's an excellent rider and takes his leadership responsibilities deeply seriously. I appreciate his commitment. We have caught up with Jeff and Steve when they hit the deepest section of mud on the road. Riding his CB500X, Jeff corkscrews first, although later I am informed that Steve on the Versey holds that honour. Either way, it's an impressive off.

Sometime later, a GoPro reel emerged, it was in the running for the best adventure riding fall of the year, if not the decade. If such an award exists. I stop when I see it unfolding; it's a synchronised effort, both riders high-siding their bikes at precisely the same time.

Dean is riding behind me on his DR650, and pulls up quickly and grabs his phone for the most essential photo opportunity of the weekend. Jeff wastes no time hauling himself out of the mud and helps Steve to do likewise, but it's too late we all managed to get photos of the incident as the recovery unfolds.

I scramble over to them, and help pick Steve's bike up. Dean was already helping Jeff and Steve clean themselves up by the time I have secured the CB500X on the road. I reached for my phone to take the vital after-shot.

If you fall off your bike, it is a given and accepted practice in the adventure riding community that, before medical treatment is administered, you are photographed. This is to show the effect of your off for further training (bragging) opportunities and post the event to social media. It also helps the coroner, should they require evidence for a later investigation.

This accident would have shaken Jeff and Steve but, if it did, they didn't show it. I follow them the entire length of the road, and for almost all of it, they are riding to the limits of their bikes. Undoubtedly, both these guys are good riders (much better than I am).

They take every good line and power through every mud pit; most of the time, I am following their line. The Versey and the CBX are more road-oriented adventure bikes, but you wouldn't know it the way these guys are riding them.

Adventure riding is a unique sport, and more and more men are getting back into bikes in this way. If there is one observation about adventure riding that I think sits above all others, it is the requirement for you to be brave, especially when shit happens. . By no means is it isolated to the male gender; it's an essential part of adventuring generally.

In adventure riding, you have a choice: slow down to the point where it's safe, but not really. Or bite the proverbial bullet and speed up. Something clicked in my mind right then. If I were going down this road, I would have to ride counterintuitively. In other words, I would have to do what I thought was counter to my own safety. I would have to ride as fast as I could.

It is an epiphany for me: riding safely does not build skills, competence or resilience. You have to ride aggressively when off-road. Only by pushing your limits and facing your fear will you become a better rider, and what better time to do it than when you are scared? A memory floods back into my consciousness.

I used to ski a lot in New Zealand; I remember skiing with an Austrian man and his son. We were members of a mountaineering club and staying in our club hut on the mountain. As usual, I was traversing across the slopes when the Austrian man skied up to me and in a firm but gentle way, he said, "Gary, if you want to ski, then turn your skis down the slope and ski aggressively or go back to the clubhouse. It's a bit like Yoda in Return of the Jedi: "Do or do not, don't try". From that time on, my skiing improved significantly. All the skills that I had developed over five years of skiing suddenly kicked in, and I found myself skiing backwards and doing tricks down some of the most adventurous black diamond runs on the mountain.

It's no different to the advice I give my daughter: close your eyes (metaphorically) if you must, as you separate the emotion from the situation and deal with what you have. My daughter had the skills; she just needed to believe she had them.

I'm about to put this wisdom to the test once again; I start to ride faster. I look up at the line ahead and, at a point in the distance, I hit one hundred kilometres per hour on the straights. Then, down to third gear, about sixty-five kilometres per hour on the muddy corners, leaning against the pull of the corner ever so slightly and back up to speed on the straights. I would be more concerned about riding fast around tight corners on the highway in this rain than on this track. The mud isn't bothering me anymore. I know Emu wants to go straight, all I have to do is let him.

As I ride down one of the more challenging straights with deep washouts and small rivers flowing across the road; two orange blurs pass me on the right side. No sooner did I register them than they were gone. Dale and Jaime pass me, doing about one hundred and twenty kilometres per hour on their KTM890s.

Dean stays behind me for most of the ride out, for which I am grateful. It's reassuring to have a buddy in such treacherous conditions. I'm sure he would have liked to have ridden faster.

Having consciously decided to ride more aggressively, I catch up to Jeff and Steve again as we get to the tar at the Lynd Roadhouse. The roadhouse is closed due to a lack of staff, so we decide to meet again for fuel and food at the Greenvale Roadhouse, which is 50 kilometres south.

We fill up our tanks at the roadhouse, paying two dollars and fifty-nine cents per litre. We grab a pie and coffee before kicking the bikes into gear and heading down the highway. After an hour and a half, we reach a monument to the Harvey Range Road. It's cold and wet, and while the heavy rain has passed, it is still a cold bone-shaking experience. I take the opportunity to put on a spare pair of bike jeans and my wet-weather jacket.

It's only one hundred kilometres to Townsville, so we say our goodbyes and head home. The only bad news is that Bob broke a chain link on his KLR and has to wait for help in the cold, rainy weather. Luckily, Dean and Barry are following Bob and stay with him until it arrived. There's a lesson for the rest of us: the ride is not over until everybody is home safe.

This adventure, more than any I've done so far, has contributed to my confidence as an adventure rider. Not only is Emu performing at the level of other more off-road tuned bikes, but I am also finally improving my confidence in riding in challenging conditions.

After the Einasleigh ride, I continue going to other group rides, each time incrementally improving my riding ability. I'm riding faster than before, averaging ninety kilometres per hour on most surfaces, leaning out of corners and keeping my line regardless of the road condition.

It's time to plan my ride to Cape York.

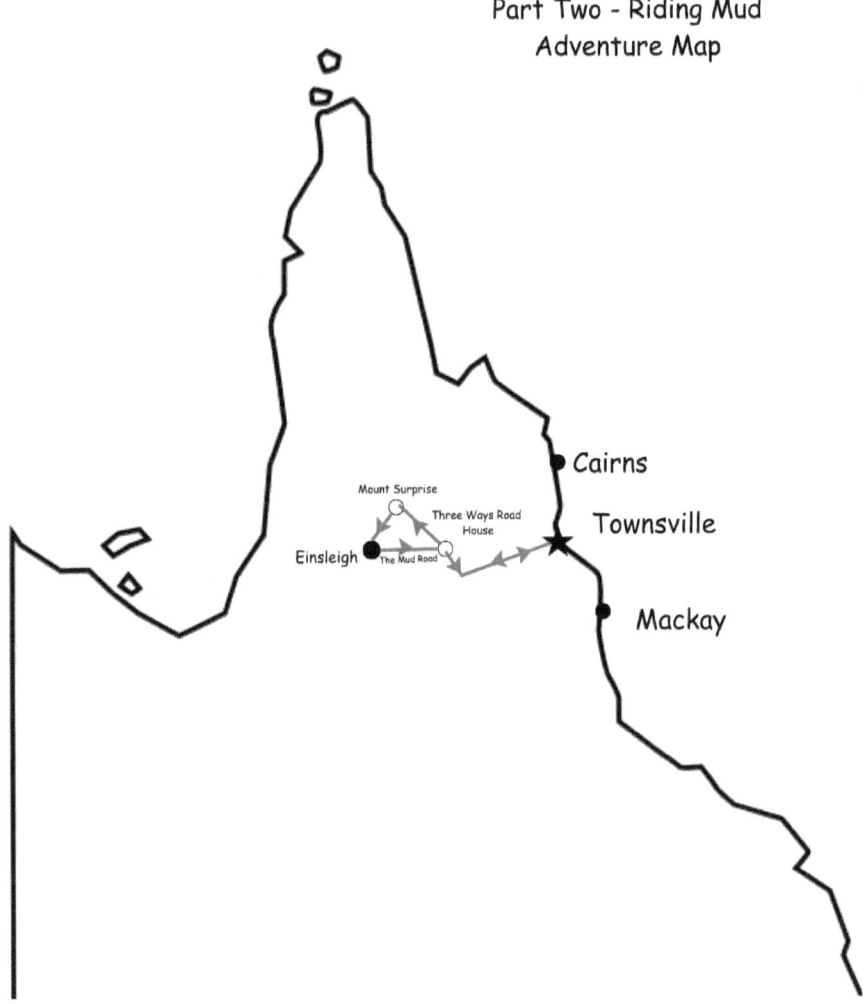

Einasleigh Hotel, Christmas in July. It's not meant to rain in North Queensland during winter.

First stop, Emu at the Three Ways Roadhouse

Einasleigh Rail Bridge at the top of Copperfield Gorge.

Copperfield Gorge

Riders arriving at the Einasleigh Waterpark, saturated ground makes camping interesting.

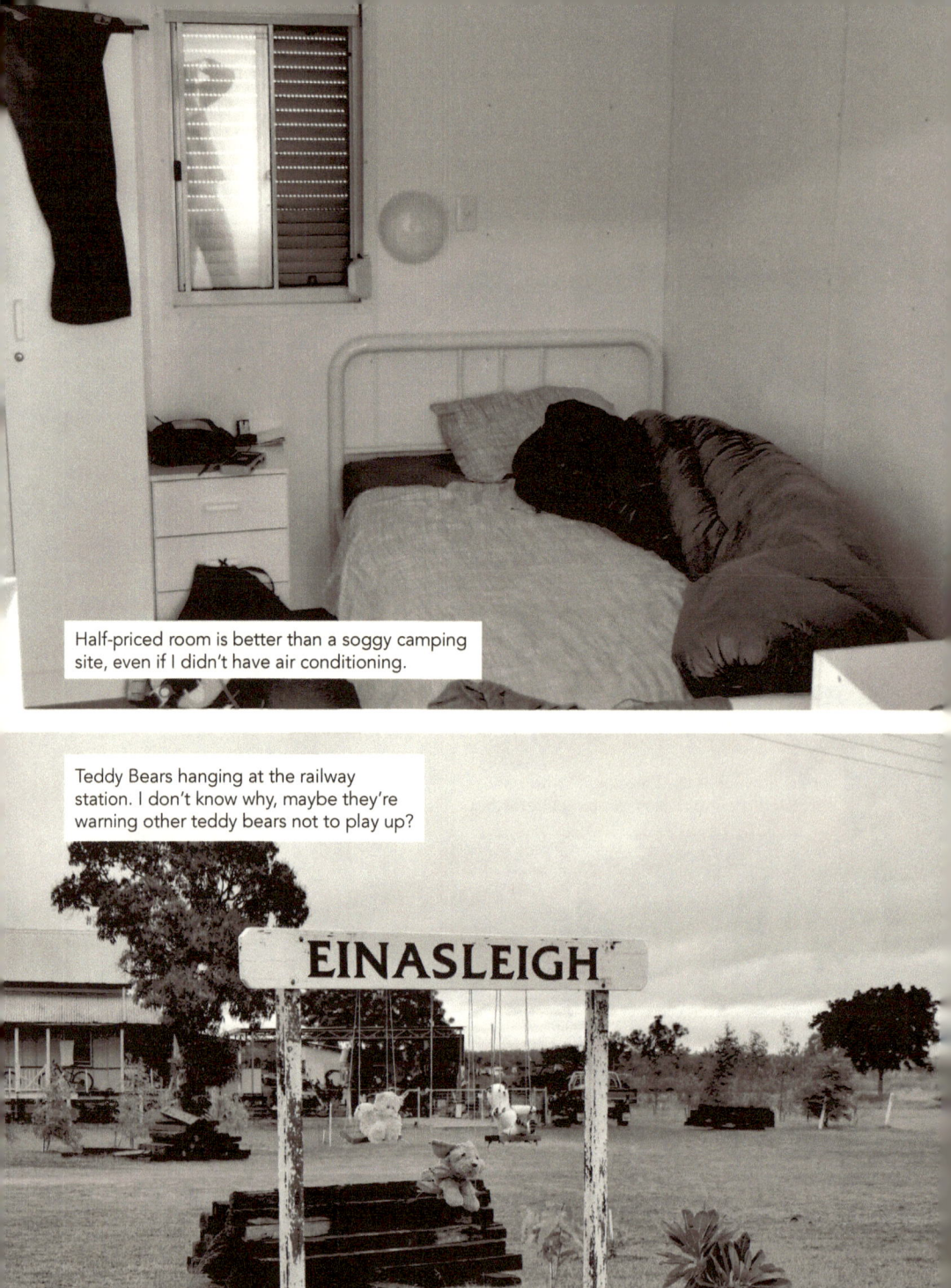

Half-priced room is better than a soggy camping site, even if I didn't have air conditioning.

Teddy Bears hanging at the railway station. I don't know why, maybe they're warning other teddy bears not to play up?

The ghostly veranda at the Einasleigh Hotel

Emu undercover just before departing

Dinner at the Einasleigh Hotel, rain still pouring down.

Riding mud can be hazardous. This was the state of most of the 80 kilometres of road, then it started raining again.

Mud incident, pulling the last bike out of the mud and taking photos for the coroner.

Crossing the Copperfield River before the mud highway.

Conjestion at the Three-Ways Roadhouse.

Assmebly at the Three-Ways after riding 80 kilometres of mud.

Chapter 21
Journey to the Northernmost Tip of Australia: Cape York

Cape York is a remote and sometimes dangerous part of the country to get to. Combined with potentially lethal animals like crocodiles and poisonous snakes, it is a must-do ride for adventure riders and four-wheel drive enthusiasts. The area is full of tracks and wild beaches to ride on, but most people ride the direct path up the Peninsula Development road, turn right at the Bamaga Road and keep going straight to the tip.

After achieving three of my bucket list items, I have become fixated on getting to the top on a motorbike. I have read books such as "King of the Cape" by Roy Kunda and Dirt and Dust by Amelia and Riley Olsen. The tip is an infatuation and my next goal, one that would test Emu and me.

A Cape York adventure is the ultimate remote travel destination. It should be on the bucket list of every adventurous Australian if you're not Australian, it will epitomise what exploring Australia is all about and how mentally tough you need to be if you want to do it by motorcycle.

Under the right conditions, your family car can travel to the northern tip of Australia. However, unless you are willing to replace all the springs, oil seals, universal joints, shock absorbers, and tyres afterwards, I would not recommend it.

The area is vast, and at times, certain conditions such as rain and flooding make it very dangerous. Not to mention the heat and humidity during the spring, summer, and autumn. Then there's the wildlife, make sure you brush up on your German.

After returning to Townsville after my death-defying mud experience, I contemplate the next great adventure. I still intend to ride around Australia, but more and more, I am drawn to the idea of riding to Cape York and standing next to the sign that signals the northernmost point on the Australian continent.

My riding ability on dirt is improving to the point I can read the road well enough to keep up with some of the more advanced riders. Emu's upgrades are working well, although he feels soft in some corners. I need to figure out why this is happening. I also upgrade his front sprocket from a fourteen to a sixteen tooth and replace the chain. Not that I needed to, but as I am going to a remote area, I didn't want to risk it breaking.

This made all the difference to his highway performance. Instead of sitting at five thousand revolutions per minute at one hundred and twenty kilometres per hour, I am now cruising at four thousand, two hundred revolutions per minute for the same speed. This means less vibration and better fuel economy. I also change the tyres again to a more off road profile.

I go to the gurus in the North Queensland Adventure Group and receive at least twenty recommendations. Eventually, I replace the Dunlop D605 and D603 tyres with Motoz Adventure Tractionators. They are designed for 30% road and 70% dirt and are perfect for a trip up Cape York. I could feel the difference when Emu was at highway speed, with less vibration and road noise.

I also buy a top-of-the-range Aria Adventure helmet and a Sena 30+ intercom system. I could listen to music and take calls while riding. This may seem dangerous until you realise you can't select music or swipe to receive a call while wearing riding gloves, so I still have to pull over when making or receiving a call.

Further refinements to Emu included RAM universal joints for mounting a set of Doubletake Adventure Mirrors. These are made of fibreglass-reinforced nylon plastic and are tough, especially if you take a fall; the mirrors fold in from multiple universal joints, and the hard glass-reinforced plastic protects the glass mirror from damage. I also purchased a standard Quad Lock to mount my phone on the handlebars.

Emu and I are ready for our adventure to the Cape, but I still have concerns about the distance and what I might expect. Then, almost as if the Universe heard me, a Facebook post came up in the North Queensland Adventure Riders Group asking if anyone wanted to go to the tip. I put my hand up (metaphorically) straight away.

The idea for this trip comes from a teenage girl (Shayla) who convinces her father that it is better and safer for her to ride a dirt bike to the tip of Cape York than to spend a week with drunken friends and sex-starved boys at schoolies week. To her credit, she didn't just evoke the protective emotions of her dad but also those of her family friend, Quentin.

As Quentin and Nick are avid off-road riders and bikers. it doesn't take too much talking for Shayla to convince them. Due to mechanical and weather conditions, neither Nick nor Quentin have reached the tip on their previous attempts.

I had considered riding it solo, but the sheer ruggedness and inaccessibility of the roads always made it seem out of reach for a solo biker. If that wasn't hard enough, it's the end of the tourist season and only weeks away from the official monsoon season called "The Wet."

No sooner had Quentin posted the idea on Facebook than six bikers signed up. We mainly communicated through Messenger and organised our intended route. We then set a date in September and agreed to meet at the Atherton Caravan Park.

In September, the weather patterns in North Australia gradually change from hot and dry to hot and wet. It stays in flux throughout the spring when the weather patterns switch to a permanent hot and wet. My adventure through the tropics in this book exemplifies what riding in the tropics is like; only going an extra one thousand kilometres north intensifies the heat even more.

The best we can hope for is a late wet season. As the humidity increases, people tend to act strangely. There's even a term for it: "Going Troppo." Going Troppo can be anything from wearing a Hawaiian shirt to dying from heat exhaustion. We hope to avoid embarrassment and, of course, death.

If the wet season starts early, the flood waters could isolate us for a few months. We would face crocodile-infested crossings if it rained enough to raise the rivers. We would have to carry bikes across and then ride down clay roads that turn into skating rinks when wet. This would make an already difficult journey into a survival situation.

As with so many of the survival stories I've read, it's always the fattest and slowest member of the group that is eaten first. A realisation that keeps me on my toes throughout the journey and vigilant to changes in weather.

A motorcycle adventure to Cape York is not to be taken lightly; any number of situations can turn into emergencies. The distances we will travel on bulldust and corrugated roads will test both the rider and the bike. From where I live in Townsville, the journey will be 2942 kilometres, with almost 2000 kilometres on the worst dirt roads in Australia.

These dirt roads are heavily corrugated, with deep holes filled with bulldust. Bulldust is fine dirt, almost like talcum powder. It hides the washouts or holes in the road. If you ride into a bulldust-covered hole, it is like riding into a deep pothole or trench. It can damage your bike or even throw you off, causing serious injuries.

It's a hot spring day, and the atmosphere is humid for this time of year. As usual, clouds linger over Mount Stuart but, to my relief and surprise, the roads out of Townsville are quiet. I arrive at Atherton Holiday Park around two thirty in the afternoon. and check into the cabin Quentin has booked for all of us.

It's not until five in the evening that Nick and Shayla arrive with their bikes on a trailer. I wonder why I didn't do the same thing and spare myself the long, hot ride. Nick and Shayla have come from Mooranbah, a coal mining town inland from Mackay.

Another group member, Flemming, has travelled from Brisbane and met our group leader, Quentin, in Rockhampton. The vehicles have some dramas, but they eventually arrive around seven o'clock.

The final member of our group is a local man who has recently retired and moved to Atherton. Rob is a tall, fit man, about sixty years old, and an avid adventure rider. We arrange to meet Rob the next day. Nick, Shayla and Quentin are old friends, but the rest of us have never met before.

That night, we get to know each other over beers and red wines. We mostly talk about bikes and adventures as we pack panniers and top bags and make last-minute adjustments to carburettors.

On day one, we meet Rob at a small cafe in the middle of Atherton. He was riding the biggest bike in the group, an Africa Twin. After introductions and a great breakfast at the cafe, we set off on our Cape York adventure.

Our bike contingent consisted of two DRZ400Es, two DR650s, a KLR650, and an Africa Twin. The DRZs are great bikes, but they tend to rev pretty high at highway speeds, making them less comfortable on the highway than on the dirt.

Chapter 22
The Journey Begins

Our mission was simple: make it to the tip and back without crashing. At the time, it's a goal that seems relatively straightforward, but later appeared overly optimistic. We mounted our bikes, hit the electric starts and listened as each, in turn, fired up.

The sound of the six bikes with modified exhausts idling simultaneously is spectacular. The locals in the streets are spinning around to see the bikie gang pass by, only to see six neatly dressed bikers riding past with fully-loaded adventure bikes.

We travel the Mulligan Highway from Mareeba to Mount Malloy, a picturesque ride along the spine of the Great Dividing Range. We pass coffee plantations and fields of avocado trees. We are riding along the Atherton Tablelands, a beautiful area reminiscent of the North Island of New Zealand. There are lush green paddocks full of dairy cows.

As we continue north, the topology changes. It becomes drier and more suited to beef cattle raising than horticulture. We eventually reach a rest area about fifty kilometres from Atherton, just past Mount Malloy.

The rest area is spacious, with well-maintained toilets and plenty of room to camp. Some grey nomads have set up their rigs behind the barbeque areas. Several fire pits, and large eucalyptus trees are around the site. It is a perfect place to wild camp.

Mount Malloy is the junction between the Atherton Hinterland and the road to Mossman and Port Douglas. If you are coming this way from Mossman, this is where you will join the Mulligan Highway to Cooktown.

As I pulled into the rest area outside, I notice something is not right with Quentin's bike. He struggles to keep it running, but it gurgles, jerks, and spits fuel everywhere. Definitely not good signs. Before I could get off my bike, Shayla demonstrated a new and unique dismount technique. It involved falling over sideways, then shimmying off her horizontal bike before getting to her feet and picking it up.

'Interesting,' I thought. Having a teenage daughter the same age as Shayla, I'm not keen to discuss it and risk retribution. Rob is the first to get to Shayla and helps her pick up the bike. I go over to where Quentin, Nick, and Flemming have pulled the carburettor off Quentin's DR650. The prognosis is that one of the main jets had worked loose and fallen out.

During times like these, I learn more about the people I'm riding with. I eventually nickname Flemming the Flying Dutchman, primarily due to his uncanny ability to ride fast and silently. Before you know it, he's motoring past you, regardless of your speed and with an effortless overtaking manoeuvre that would make Mick Doohan envious (Doohan was an Australian 500cc World Champion).

But with his meticulous, understated attention to detail, he notices the jet sitting in a groove in the engine, along with its locking washer and spring. How the parts stay in that position and how he spots them is still a mystery. It takes some time to remove and reassemble the offending parts. Before long, the engine is running again, and we are ready for the next stage of our journey.

The road to Lakeland is a spectacular ride through eucalyptus forests and dense tropical scrub, typical of the iconic Australian bush. Before long, it opens up into a dryer, more sparse grassland. We settle into a group riding configuration, with four of us connected via our wireless headsets.

It took us some time the night before to get these headsets working, but luckily, we have our very own Gen Z superstar to make it happen. Without Shayla's expertise, we wouldn't have been communicating at all. Every bike adventure group should have a Gen Z for such occasions. So, while her motorcycle dismounting technique left much to be desired, her ability to get the intercom app working is genius.

The Mulligan Highway to Cooktown starts to flatten out into grassland and, as such, come out of the shade of tall trees around the almost ghost town of Mount Carbine. From then on, we're in cattle country and the heat increases. The wind is keeping us cool, but there's no doubt this will be a hot trip. The temperature is starting to hit 35 degrees Celsius.

Keeping as cool as possible will be a significant safety factor on this trip. Therefore, I forego the usual heavy adventure jacket and Kevlar-lined jeans for a lighter ensemble. I have purchased a body armour vest, an elastic open-weave, zip-up shirt with CE body armour sewn into all the right places. I also buy a pair of nylon motocross pants with Kevlar lining and leather inserts at all the wear points, such as the thighs, knees and hips.

Under the shirt, I wear my Marino tee shirt. Initially, I am wearing my motocross shirt over this ensemble. Still, as the days wear on and the temperature rises, I am less concerned about fashion and far more concerned about keeping cool. I stow my motocross shirt and allow the breeze to flow through my body armour lining.

Flemming and Rob wear a similar setup; Quentin has on a light adventure jacket and jeans while Nick and Shayla wear full adventure jackets and pants. By the second day, Rob and Flemming wore their body armour vests with no shirts underneath.

In the distance, I see the shimmering outline of the Byerstown Range; it's not long before we're winding up the range. The KLR loves this type of terrain, and I found lying into the corners a relief from the long, flat road behind us.

About halfway up the range, we come across a small area on the right to pull over and enjoy the "Bob's Lookout" view. The views are stunning. As I look over the semi-arid, dry tropics landscape, I imagine the early European settlers and what they must have endured. It's an excellent opportunity for us to have a break and cool down.

Have you ever wondered about the stupidity of signs? As we approach the lookout, there is a sign indicating no right turn; in other words, keep going for another fifty kilometres, do a U-turn at the Palmer River Roadhouse and return. Ignoring the stupid sign, we turn right, avoiding the non-existent traffic coming the other way and park our bikes facing uphill.

I'm intrigued as to who Bob was and why they named this lookout after him. When I'm doing some research for this book, I find more information:

***

In 1873, Norman Hann and William Taylor discovered gold at the confluence of Prospect and Campbell Creeks, approximately the current Palmer River Roadhouse site. This led to one of Queensland's (and Australia's) biggest gold rushes.

Eventually, a track was formed from Cooktown to Palmer River, but not without violence and the killing of many Aboriginal people. It was reported that Aboriginal warriors attacked the expedition party, and they were forced into a pitched battle.

The warriors were routed and pursued; many were killed. This area became known as "Battle Camp." The gold prospectors' track was called Battle Camp

Road and is still used today to access the old Laura township and the Lakeland National Park.

The violence and killing didn't go one way only. There are many reports of mass killings by Aboriginal people against European and Chinese miners.

***

I'm grateful that, as a modern adventurer, I'm not faced with hostile Aborigines or crazy gold prospectors, just bouncing bloody Kangaroos.

After a brief respite from the road and several photos later, we return to adventure riding. While we would have liked to stop at Palmer River Roadhouse, we want to make some distance. We decide to refuel in Lakeland before heading up to Hann River Roadhouse for the night.

The roadhouse at Lakeland (Lakeland Downs) is a busy stop-off for tourists visiting the Cape, especially at this time of year. It's at the junction of the Peninsula Development Road (PDR) and the Mulligan Highway to Cooktown. On one side of the bowser, we note the fresh, clean vehicles, while on the other, the four-wheel drives are covered in red dirt.

Likewise, the drivers of the fresh, clean cars are decidedly less harassed than their red dirt counterparts. Before the end of this adventure, we will be able to empathise with those covered in red dirt and looking relieved

Upon arriving, I refuel Emu and look for a shady resting place. It's midday, the sun is beating directly down on us, and the only place I can find is tucked behind the roadhouse. I could gain a small amount of shade by sticking close to the building structure.

Shayla demonstrated her dismount technique; this time, I had my camera out. Considering the traffic conditions, I feel her technique might be dangerous, so I take it upon myself to show her an alternative: by standing on the peg opposite the side stand and counterbalancing, then pivoting onto the bike, taking most of her weight on the right side of the bike and reducing any pressure on the stand. I easily twist my left leg over my back bag when I demonstrate it.

She takes the advice gracefully and is soon flicking on and off her bike like a seasoned professional adventure rider.

Chapter 23
The Peninsula Development Road (PDR)

The Peninsula Development Road (PDR) runs from Lakeland Downs, where we are currently, to Weipa, a distance of five hundred and seventy kilometres. It's the main access road to Cape York. Generally, when people think of travelling to Cape York, they assume the original road to be the Old Telegraph Track (OTT), but this is not the case. To access the OTT, you must first drive up the PDR as far as the Bramwell Junction Roadhouse.

Fuelled, fed and recovered, we are all keen to get back on the road and get some air flowing through our jackets. The heat is building, and the day is waning. I am hoping to make it to the Hann River Roadhouse before four in the afternoon to avoid any entanglements with my nemesis: Skippy, the bush kangaroo.

The petrol attendant informs us that a 31-year-old biker died yesterday while on an organised bike tour of the Cape. He hit a wallaby near the "Five Beaches," lost control of his bike and hit a tree. It's always a tragedy when a person dies like this.

You feel it more when you're a biker and a parent (RIP, young adventurer). When we hear about the death of this young rider, we discuss the incident and remind ourselves that it is important to keep control of our bikes and brace for impact and, if needed, hit the kangaroo or wallaby head-on.

Our first stop is the town of Laura, established in 1873 after Archibald Macmillan explored the area and named the river after his wife. It became a central staging post for miners during the Palmer River Gold Rush. The area's significance goes back further for the local Aboriginal people, who are custodians of a rich collection of Aboriginal rock art, highlighting their connection with the land.

New Laura stands at the intersection of Battle Camp Road and the PDR. In its early years, old Laura was twenty-seven kilometres west of the current Laura township. At the time, it was the main track for miners disembarking from Cooktown on their way to the Palmer River gold diggings. The road to Laura is sealed, making it a fast run to the town.

Along the way, we pass banana farms and, later, significant cattle stations. After an hour, we arrived at Laura and pull into the grandest building in the town, the Cultural Centre. We make ourselves a coffee and explore the camping area which is not very appealing. Thoughts of pulling up for the night evaporated after we take a look at the dusty, dry ground.

We are keen to continue our journey before the sun starts to set, so we leave Laura at about three in the afternoon. Nick is having problems starting his bike, so we give him a push start—a sign of an issue that would stay with Nick for the entire journey.

Leaving Laura, we ride past the Old Laura Road which joins with Battle Camp Road and Lakefield National Park. It would have been great to explore this area, but the objective of our adventure was Cape York, so we continued. We all agreed we would have to make another trip to explore this area and possibly have a beer at the pub.

After about fifty kilometres, we come upon our first section of dirt road. While it only lasts about twenty kilometres, it is some of the deepest bulldust I had ever ridden. On top of that are the bone-shattering corrugations, a tantalising taste of what's to follow.

A four-wheel drive with a camper trailer is parked on the side of the road, with the occupants letting down their tyre pressure. I thought it was a bit premature, but I'm not there to judge other people's strategy.

I am refocusing on the road when a small wallaby tore across in front of me; I hit the back brake hard and feathered the front. I would miss it, but it's going to be close. I miss his tail by about one and a half metres; at ninety kilometres per hour, it's a near miss.

I keep braking until the wallaby is well off the road; you never know with kangaroos and wallabies; they can decide to swing back at you, or there might be another one on the side of the road, waiting to kill itself and seriously injure you. Usually, roos come in pairs, so you're always on edge once you see one. I let everyone know over the intercom.

My near-miss is a wake-up call for all of us. Not only would the corrugated bulldust road be a challenge, but we also have to scan constantly for wildlife.

The tar road reappears about five kilometres out of the Hann River Roadhouse. It has been a long day. As the signage and narrow bridge over the Hann River appeared, my spirits lifted. Finally, my adventure is beginning in earnest.

Our priorities are to have some cold beers, find a campsite, and cook something for dinner. We sit around putting our tents up and getting to know each other better over a few cold beers. I was approached by a man in an old Land Cruiser. He's wearing a tattered Akubra hat and has a bushy beard.

His tanned, leathery face indicates he's in his sixties. "Gidday, mate, do youse want to come down to the wallaby feeding?" he said enthusiastically in a broad Queensland accent.

I genuinely thought it was an offer to come to a barbecue. "We're not sure what we're doing for dinner yet," I said, "I've never eaten wallabies. What do they taste like"?

"Nah, nah, he said, "We don't eat them, mate; we feed them. They come around every evening to be fed."

"Mate, why do you want to feed the fuckers?" I asked. "There's too many on the road as it is. I almost hit one on the way in here." He is perplexed by my response. At which point he jumps back into the driver's seat of his cruiser and leaves. I still don't know what I said to offend him. It wasn't until later in the trip, when I told this story to the others, that Nick put his hand on his head and rolled back in laughter. "So that's why the guy was so cold towards us!" "Gary wanted to eat his pets".

The day has been successful. We had met as a group of strangers and, by the end of the day, we had become friends. We'd shared some great riding and a few laughs, learnt new techniques for getting off our bikes, and now we were settling into our camps for the night.

Chapter 24
Corrugations and Bulldust

"When I'm riding my motorcycle, I'm glad to be alive. When I stop riding my motorcycle, I'm glad to be alive."

- Neil Peart

The bulldust and corrugations are intense, and just as I am questioning my rationale for riding this horrendous road, things get much worse. I come across a car overtaking another on the inside of the table drain. The right-side wheels of the overtaking car ultimately leave the road. The car twists over the top edge of the table drain and falls back into the bulldust. The dust covers it completely, but it punches through the cloud like a surfer punching through the back of a wave.

The camper trailer swings side-on towards me before it falls in line behind the car, burying itself in the dust. For a moment, I thought, 'It's all over.' The vehicle being overtaken is doing about 90 kph, a reasonable speed considering the state of the road. The Toyota Land Cruiser overtaking on the inside table drain is doing over one hundred and fifty kilometres per hour, and the driver is totally out of control.

I have nowhere to go, and I can't stop. My only chance to survive is to swing wide and high on a corrugated corner and into the bulldust. I am steeling myself for a lot of pain. Even though the corrugations shake every part of my body, I am lucky that the corner was formed so far as to have a high climbing camber. I manage to stop at the top and take deep hard breaths of air (and dust) to calm my fractured nerves.

The day didn't start this dramatically, but it soon becomes apparent road rules normal people consider reasonable didn't apply to redneck four-wheel drivers on the PDR. This scenario would play out in different incidents during our ride to the tip and back.

The day starts very pleasantly with my first cup of coffee and breakfast. A blistering hot day yesterday but it has cooled overnight, and dew is covering the tents. Slowly, everybody wakes from their slumber and, one by one, I watch our riding group emerge.

Quentin and I stroll around, trying to figure out where the earth tremors are coming from. Shayla can be heard snoring, which prompts us to nickname her 'the bear,' and we refer to her tent as 'the bear cave.' Nick, some distance away, could also be heard. She told us she stayed away from Nick because of his snoring. Go figure. When Nick and Shayla wake up and emerge, the tremors stop. Coincidence?

I walk to the river to see if I can spot and photograph a crocodile, but all I see is a well-fed wallaby. The creek is tranquil, but we have been warned it is home to man-eating crocodiles. This dangerous creek is surrounded by tropical plants that filter the light into soft green rays.

It flows gently over rocks, forming small waterfalls that cascade into shallow pools of water. Although this is hardly the environment for crocodiles, you can never be sure in the Australian tropics. If only I knew more German, I could coax them out.

The campground is pleasant and the resident birds make you feel like you are in a nature reserve. Peahens, peacocks, and guinea fowl wander around as if they own the place and a resident poddy cow is corralled in a small pen near the roadhouse for children to play with.

Water is an issue on the PDR; not every campground has drinking water, so you must fill your dehydration packs with bottled water. As I'm purchasing water, some travellers who have come down from the top are having breakfast.

"What's the road like ahead?" I ask. "Ohh mate, It's bad, really bad; look out for the yellow sand; it's hiding deep holes, and the corrugation will kill you if you hit them square on," he said, screwing up his face as if he's suffering a pain in his gut.

"Is it worse than what we went through from Laura?" I asked.

"Ohh mate, it's a hundred times worse," replied our travel guide from the north.

I don't know what Quentin thought, but I am wondering if this adventure is a good idea. One hundred times worse sounds pretty extreme, and what's this yellow sand that creeps up on you as you ride?

The roads to the Cape are wide which belies the fact that only a portion of the road is usable. For a bike, this is reduced even further to one or two lines on each side. The lines are where the dust, sand or gravel has been pushed aside or worn away. The ground is usually harder at these points, enabling a more even surface to ride on. But if you go either side of these lines, the bulldust is quite deep and makes your front wheel slide slightly.

When these roads are worn or damaged by too much traffic, the holes get more profound, filling with soft dust and masking the deep holes underneath them. This dust has very little consistency and no resistance. That's why it's called bulldust.

You can usually see bulldust patches before you hit them, which gives you time to brace, drop down a gear or choose another line to travel. If you don't see them, that's when disaster strikes.

Hitting bulldust is inevitable; sometimes, the dust or sand is too thick across the road to avoid or your concentration wanders momentarily. At times like these, you have to believe in your bike, and as Rob said, "Your bike wants to go straight; let it do its job." This is excellent advice, but your bike must be set up correctly.

Unfortunately, I find that mine is not. On these roads at any speed over eighty kilometres per hour, the back end starts to jump around and slip sideways. It has the effect of pulling the front out of the line I set for it. The result is terrifying, and I have to wrestle with the bike to keep the front wheel straight.

It isn't until much later in the trip, when we are discussing the road conditions that I learn all our team members are fighting their own battles with the road.

I am finding some of the worst bulldust and corrugations are on the uphill side of corners. The edges are deep in bulldust, and the corrugations are horrendous. Riding these corners, we must come into the lower part of the corner fairly hot and accelerate in a straight line. It's an ideal scenario for the KLR, as most of its torque is in the lower rev range.

It means I have most of my control in the lower revs; a 650 twin would need to be revving a lot higher to achieve the same torque, making for a challenging exit from the corner in an attempt to stop the wheels from spinning. The only problem is the cars and trucks coming the other way; when this occurs, there's a mad scramble to the uphill position and a slight and unnerving loss of control.

There is evidence of wrecked vehicles and caravans often up the road. The reasons vehicles come to grief on these roads are twofold: one, not driving to the conditions or, two, a poorly set up caravan with the wrong weight distribution. I pass a large caravan on the side of the road, slowly being pulled apart by people looking for spare parts. Further up the road, we come across a wrecked caravan loaded onto the back of a truck.

Our group settles into a formation with Quentin in the lead, followed by Rob, then me, Shayla and Nick. Flemming would start at the back and, by about halfway, become bored and whistle past all of us, hence the nickname the "Flying Dutchman". The big Africa Twin soaks up the corrugations like a train on rails, and eventually, Rob moved to the front.

Emu and I are not handling the bulldust and corrugations very well. I put it down to my anxiety over the road. I realise, however, that I've travelled 18,000 kilometres on Emu and am a moderately experienced rider. It's the problem I identified before, the back of the bike pulling the front out of line.

This causes me to look down in front of the bike to see what the front wheel is doing rather than looking up and picking the correct line in the distance. I constantly adjust for the immediate landscape rather than choosing the best line. Not a good riding technique.

The exact cause wouldn't become evident until the second last day of our adventure. Needless to say, about halfway to Coen, Shayla, sick of my changing speed, decides sitting behind me is too painful and went flying past. She eventually makes it to the front and jostles Rob for pole position.

The roads have to be ridden relatively fast to maintain consistency and cover the required distances. My only advantage is on the tar where I redeem myself and catch up to almost everybody. The KLR is a better-handling bike on the tar and could easily reach speeds of one hundred and forty kilometres per hour (if needed). The downside is that it uses more fuel at these speeds. Luckily, fuel isn't an issue with petrol stations every one hundred and fifty kilometres apart.

About thirty kilometres out of Coen, the road is sealed, making the ride into town more relaxing. Rob waits at the entrance to town and shows me the way to the general store and petrol station. We refuel our bikes and have a sandwich from the local store before looking around for a place to sit and relax.

There's not much infrastructure for tourists and limited food options at the petrol station, but the local hotel has more food and beverages. It is called the "SEexchange Hotel." Local tradies fixing the roof decided to add an "S" in front of the Exchange Hotel sign, thinking the name would probably bring in more customers. No one objected, and it was adopted.

Coen was established as a fort to protect gold prospectors after discovering gold in the area in 1876. The gold didn't last long, with about one thousand six hundred and seventy kilograms extracted over the lifetime of the mining operations. Significant gold mining activity was eventually shut down in 1916 with the closure of the Great Northern Mine.

However, smaller gold operators remained active until the 1930s. Coen became a vital staging post during the Second World War, and today, it's a support town for travellers to Weipa and the local agricultural community.

Nick is still having trouble starting his bike. It takes a while, but he, Quentin, and Flemming eventually solve the issues. Rob, Shayla and I, who were of no use to the others, go for a walk around the town. It's hot and dry; the grass is a greenish-brown colour and, in many areas, it stands over a metre high; the houses are more like shacks than urban brick and tile dwellings. There are many government departments clustered together into service centres.

We eventually return to the small barn we had found to keep the sun off the mechanics as they worked. We found a big shady tree out back of the barn sheds and sat under it, trying to keep cool. A young Aboriginal truck driver came over and asked if we were OK. He has a cousin who can fix bikes. We only need to get the bike to Bamaga.

Eventually, we heard the purring sound of Nick's bike, then a splutter, and it stopped. We all fell back against the tree until we heard Nick calling out for us to give him a push. The problem was temporarily fixed but, unfortunately, to fully rectify the problem would require significant work which wasn't possible on the trip.

Nick figured out a process for starting the bike that would make us all much fitter over the coming days. By banding together and pushing, we were back on the road.

The next part of our journey is over two hundred kilometres, passing some of the Cape's most iconic areas. Our destination was the Bramwell Junction Roadhouse, not to be confused with Bramwell Tourist Park (Rob). We would lose one of our numbers before we arrive.

About twelve riders pass on CRF450s as we rode out of town. This is a necessary staging and refuel place for tour operators. I wondered how these bikes coped with the long bulldust and corrugated roads. Without gear, they were significantly lighter than we were. However, the good thing about a big single-engine 650 is that it keeps thumping away.

The road to Archer River is mainly tar-sealed, with minor dirt sections. The topology of the land changes and, on the dirt sections, we encounter the occasional sandy patch.

Archer River Roadhouse is only sixty five kilometres from Coen. What a surprise to come across a traffic light! As an example of the slow but methodical upgrading of the PDR, road gangs, water trucks, and graders are working on the road.

You could be excused for thinking it was the centre of Brisbane with the complexity of earthworks. We all marvel at the crystal clear waters of the Archer River as we wait for the red light to change. The desire to jump in and cool off in those crystal clear waters is overwhelming.

We raced past the turn-off to Lockhart River and, within no time at all, we reach the intersection between the PDR and Telegraph Road. The PDR would continue to Weipa. We turned right to follow the Telegraph Road to the Bramwell Junction Roadhouse, where it splits into the Old Telegraph Track and the Bamaga Road to the Cape, and the fast-flowing tar-sealed road instantly turned to bulldust and corrugations.

Clearly, the next one hundred and fourteen kilometres would be more brutal. There are more bulldust and corrugations, and even the tiny, innocuous termite mounds are more significant. We are now baking in the afternoon's heat, and we have been riding all day. The road is quickly deteriorating, as is my energy.

It's a good time to take a break, collect my thoughts, and refocus on the riding ahead. We stop at the Moreton Telegraph Station; Shayla, Flemming, and Quentin are waiting for the rest of us. I am the last to turn up. By this time, the others are ready to continue. With more time available, this would have been a fantastic place to stop for the night and explore.

The road to Bramwell Junction Roadhouse, as opposed to Bramwell Tourist Park (Rob), turns out to be one of the worst roads we had ridden. It's getting late, and the afternoon sun is casting those zebra-like shadows across the road.

Several massive holes stretch across the road in addition to the dangerous bulldust and corrugations. Some of the holes are over a metre and a half deep. Deep sections of yellow and white sandy bulldust holes appear on the ridges. In the corners, the corrugations are small speed bumps. The risks of going too fast and hitting one of the holes or a roo jumping out at you have increased significantly.

The journey feels never-ending over some of the worst roads in Queensland. Eventually, I hit tar about five kilometres out of Bramwell Junction Roadhouse. It has been four hundred and ten kilometres of what, at times, was over smooth-riding tar-sealed highway, but, for the greater part, is over the most brutal bulldust and corrugations I have ever ridden.

There was a sign to the right for the Bramwell Tourist Park; I am not sure if it's our destination for the night, but as I couldn't see any of the others, , I ride on. Soon, a long sweeping corner comes into view, and in front of me is a petrol bowser. Shayla and Nick are filling their bikes for the next leg. This is where we are camping tonight.

The camping facilities are basic: a toilet, a shower, green grass, and plenty of drinkable water. I refill my water bladder in my backpack and take out my tent. My camp set-up includes my Heliox chair and table, food supply, cooking gear, and thongs.

Pulling off my riding boots, I walk into the roadhouse in my socks to order a beer. I return to my chair, put my feet on my small collapsible table and relax. I thought to myself, 'This was the worst of it. Tomorrow, we will take a short, easy ride to Bamaga and then ride to the tip.

Chapter 25
The Road Less Travelled

> The road less travelled is synonymous with taking the hard road and growing spiritually. Goldsmith's quote says it all: "Life is a journey that must be travelled no matter how bad the roads and accommodations."
>
> - Oliver Goldsmith

The morning is crisp. I'm lying under my down quilt, looking up at the green tinge coming from my tent fly. It's cool, and I've had a good night's sleep. I can see the sun is starting to rise, so I crawl out of my tent and put on the Jetboil to make my morning coffee. Over the road, there is a giant ant nest, about four metres high and a meter and a half thick. It's a dull, oche-brown colour.

I sit with my legs on my table and my coffee in hand. I don't feel the euphoric sense of achievement I would normally have for such an adventure. If I'm honest, my knees hurt from the braces, and my shoulders are getting sore from the stress of trying to keep Emu in one direction. But I do have a dogged determination to get to the tip. It's the destination that's driving me now. I've noticed throughout my life that it's times like these that make me stronger. They test me to the limit, it's easy to give up and say, "Well, at least I tried". But when I have a burning goal, some inner strength kicks in and I keep going. I remember once climbing the glacier on Mount Ruapehu in New Zealand. It was getting dark, and we had limited time to get to the top; there was an ice ridge we had to climb. It was only 100 metres high, but that seemed like an unachievable goal in my state of tiredness and fatigue; each step was a torturous agony. My climbing buddies and I had to cut steps with our ice axes.

I remember my climbing buddy saying, "Don't focus on the ridge, just kick one step at a time. It was one of those life lessons. I think about that day on the ice every time I want to give up—just one more step. The view from the ice ridge looking down into the crater lake with the bright orange sky turning to an inky blue and the full moon rising is a moment that will stay with me forever. Was it worth the effort-shit yeah.

The sun is turning the sky a pinky-brown colour, reflecting the dust in the atmosphere. At this moment, I don't think our achievements over the past couple of days have sunk in. We have all endured, having pushed ourselves hard to keep ourselves and our bikes going. We have experienced the most horrendous riding conditions. The last thing on my mind now is to contemplate what an outstanding achievement this has been. It won't be until I'm standing on the tip that I appreciate what a monumental achievement this has been.

As I watch the termite mound change from dull brown to fluorescent terracotta, the sky is bright blue, and the sun's rays cast a golden glow across the campsite. It's only brief, but I get that wonderful feeling of a Moment when the world knits together all of its spectacular elements and nature reveals itself.

As adventure riders, we always seek the road less travelled, but I wonder if we are really seeking moments like this one that bring us closer to nature. Maybe it's why people come up this way and why it's such a bucket list item for many, including myself. A place to go that is challenging but with tremendous rewards.

It isn't easy to get here, but I can't help feeling that if the road was sealed to the tip, it would lose its character. Would the people making the trip today be the same type of people making it tomorrow?

I feel lucky to make this trip now while the terrain is still challenging. The road to the tip is often confused with the Old Telegraph Track (OTT). The OTT is the most direct way to the tip from here but is also the most challenging track. It hasn't been maintained since the bypass was built and is the ultimate four-wheel drive challenge.

There are colossal drop-offs into every creek bed, no bridges and crocodile-infested rivers. Attempting the OTT with fully-loaded adventure bikes might be too much, but we feel we should at least see what all the hype was about. We will attempt the OTT or at least part of it today.

The Bamaga Road leads north, bathed in the golden light of a new day. I wonder how many people have considered taking the Cape trip but decided not to because it seemed too difficult or remote.

The first birds are making their early morning calls, and a loud, synchronous snoring can be heard across the campground. Yesterday afternoon, we met a couple, Kyle and Deb, and their daughter, Kirra. They have just come down the OTT and will be making their way home today. Kyle and Deb are experienced four-wheel drivers, so we asked about road and track conditions.

They assure us that the creek crossings on the OTT are very low, and we wouldn't have problems getting the bikes across them. Kyle's only warning is that Palm Creek, the first creek we will come to, is quite steep, but if you can get across that one, the rest would be easy.

A little later, we talk with another couple who had driven down the Bamaga Road. They are less enthusiastic. "Mate, the bulldust holes will swallow you guys; look out for the big yellow patches; you'll disappear into them," he said.

At this point, his wife Annette commented, "Mate, the corrugations are huge; don't risk it if you can go up the OTT."

It became clear that the quality of road advice varied between different types of travellers, and none of it was beneficial. I guess I was only looking for someone to say, "It's great, easy, and you'll have no problems." A reassurance that all would be OK. But the reality is it's a shit road, and that's what makes this an adventure. If it were easy, everybody would be doing it.

During breakfast, we discuss the idea of going up the OTT. After all, if the Bamaga Road is so bad, there is nothing to lose. We agree to ride to the first creek crossing and, if we managed to get through it, we will continue on to Fruit Bat Falls. We can then complete our journey on the Northern Bypass Road.

Rob is found early the next day when the sweet sound of his 1050 cc twin adventure machine hums into the petrol bowser. He turned off at the Bramwell Tourist Park and booked in before we arrived at the roadhouse. He spent the night having a singalong with fellow grey nomads, talking extensively about arthritis and pension plans. It's a shame we missed out on that, it would have been fun:(

Rob arrives at the roadhouse as we are finishing packing our gear. He is on hand to assist Quentin and Nick with their new method of starting the ailing DRZ. Have you ever seen those memes on Facebook where it says, "Why do women live longer than men?"

I don't know about the merits of running two bikes back to back, with one trying to spin the wheel of the other to crash-start it. Still, you have to try these things at least once in your life. It looked good on YouTube.

As I walk to the shop for a drink, I pass the seven people trying to start Nick's bike; I'm minding my own business when I'm set upon by "Bottomly Potts." If you don't know, Bottomly Potts is one of the characters in the children's book

"Hairy Maclary of Donaldson's Dairy." The story is about a gang of miscreant dogs. I couldn't work out what I did to offend the little fellow!

He is aggressive and persistent and wouldn't let me in the shop until the owner came out, at which time butter wouldn't melt in the little shit's mouth. I feel like giving it a good kick up the arse; I'm sure I'm not the only one thinking the same thing.

So that you know, the bike didn't start with this new technique, and we end up push-starting it. It looked so easy on YouTube.

A feature of this part of the track is the giant termite mounds. There are some excellent examples opposite and around the roadhouse. We stop to take a group photo next to one; how often can you find a bright red termite mound that is four metres tall?

The OTT used to be the only track from this point to Cape York. It was regularly maintained until two bypass sections of the road were built in 1986. These became known as the Southern and Northern Bypass Roads. Riding the OTT is the straightest line to the Cape.

However, it is no longer maintained and is subject to a lot of four-wheel drive traffic, resulting in its condition deteriorating to the point where even gentle creek entries have become vertical challenges. A great example of this deterioration is the legendary "Gun Shot," with its four-metre vertical drop into a muddy trench with vertical walls.

Something about the name "Old Telegraph Track" elicits a feeling of adventure. We've all seen the insane antics of would-be four-wheel-driving heroes dropping $80,000 vehicles vertically down narrow embankments into pits of mud, only to be winched out, scraping their side panels and bending bull bars.

Or where teams of bikers have waded neck-deep in crocodile-infested rivers to carry bikes across.

People refer to the OTT as a single track, but it is divided into two sections. The first, or southern, section starts outside the Bramwell Junction Roadhouse where we intend to ride today. The second, or northern, section starts at Fruit Bat Falls. It continues onto the old Jardine River crossing which has been closed due to crocodiles eating people and expensive abandoned four-wheel drives choking up the pristine river system.

The first section of the track to Palm Creek crossing is your typical single-track riding, with its up jumps, tight corners, sand and technical manoeuvring required of the bike. Emu handles this well, even though he is loaded with luggage. It takes a bit of feathering the clutch and the appropriate application of power for the sandy sections.

A couple of times, in the deeper sand, I lose the front wheel, but I manage to keep the bike under control by transferring my weight from side to side. The other team members have similar issues, and Rob drops the big Africa Twin several times. It takes some heaving and pushing to lift it out of the sand and up onto harder ground.

When we reach the first creek, everyone is breathing hard and sweating profusely. The dry, hot air and the lack of breeze due to the low scrub and the tight track are causing the bikes and riders to overheat.

It's also challenging to build up speed in the sandy sections. While it wouldn't be difficult for the smaller bikes to ride the OTT, with a fully loaded adventure bike and no breeze to cool us down, we could potentially get heat exhaustion. The bikes are far too heavy to throw around on a single track for hours.

Palm Creek poses a problem for the adventure bikes because the entry was a sheer vertical trench, approximately three metres high. We find a way around the entry, but it would be challenging to get the fully loaded adventure bikes down into and then out of the creek.

I am confident I could ride down what they call the "chicken track," (clearly named by a poultry farmer), because from where I am sitting on Emu at the top, it's far from an easy alternative. I decide to walk down and check out the base of the drop. I could ride down it, but would drop the bike in the sandy creek once I got to the bottom. There's no way I could control Emu and turn the front wheel once he hit the sandy bottom with all the weight the bike is carrying pushing down on us.

If we went down, it, I'm fairly confident I could ride him back out. I have ridden more demanding tracks on my parents-in-law's cattle property and in the mud. Getting out looks easier than getting in. However, once we get them out, we still don't know if riding the track in this heat and humidity is safe.

In the end, we decide that our goal is to get to the tip without crashing. The OTT is not part of our plan for this journey, so we ride back to Bramwell Junction and start up the southern and northern bypass roads. The OTT now stands out more as a road less travelled because it's unachievable this time. We agree to return with support vehicles and lighter bikes to ride it, maybe in the middle of winter.

We have lost a couple of hours at Palm Creek; it's now ten in the morning, and we have a fair bit of road to ride.

The tar finishes about 500 metres north of the roadhouse. From this point on, it's all bulldust and corrugations. Our adventure is getting to the pointy end, literally; we are now riding the road less travelled. The dirt is in good condition at the start, and the riding is quite fast and enjoyable. It wouldn't stay that way for long.

Unexpectedly, we soon ride through the rainforest on a deep red dirt road. Not only is it pleasant to be surrounded by the lush greenery, but it is also decidedly cooler. We enjoy the much-needed break from the direct sunlight.

As we emerge from the rainforest onto the ridge line, the road condition deteriorates significantly. The winding corners are full of sharp, unforgiving corrugations. Deep bulldust holes lie between the corners and on the straights. I struggle to guide the front wheel straight as the bulldust covers the roads and hides the lines.

The holes are extensive and easy to see. They tend to be yellow or white, and smooth against the corrugated terracotta soil. These must be the car-swallowing yellow bulldust patches mentioned by our guide at Hann River Roadhouse and by Ken and Annette at Bramwell. I'm able to avoid them on a motorbike, but cars have no way of avoiding them, especially at speed.

Several wheel tracks are ploughed into the table drains, and I find myself marvelling at the stupidity of some drivers racing to overtake. As I approach a corner on top of the ridge, I encountered a Toyota Land Cruiser and camper trailer overtaking a smaller four-wheel drive (this is the incident I discussed at the beginning of this section).

After this near-death experience, I ride past the track to the Highland Ranger Station which has a sandy path into Gun Shot. It would have been interesting to go in and examine the carnage, but I am focused on getting to Fruit Bat Falls to cool off.

The road widens, and I can see the sign to Fruit Bat Falls. It signals the Southern Bypass's end and the Northern OTT's beginning. I feel immense relief to see the rest of the group waiting at the turn-off. We ride the sandy track to the car park together where we are met by bikini-clad girls and boys in board shorts. It's a strange contrast to my dirty biker clothing, boots and body armour.

I find a park near a locked gate and proceed to get out of my riding gear and remove my armour. It is a short walk past the toilet block to steps leading down onto a rock flat. In front of me is the magnificent Fruit Bat Falls, a broad four-metre-high rock wall where the water of millennia has carved a series of waterfalls from the rock. The water flows squarely over the entire sixty-metre-wide rock ledge. In three spots, the water has carved out narrow gullies that have become crashing waterfalls.

The water has a green tinge and is calm in places, clear and turbulent near the waterfalls. It has a rocky bottom with occasional rock bommie hidden from view. I didn't bring my thongs down to protect my toes. The air is thick with curses as I constantly locate each bommie by jamming my toe into it. The falls provide the perfect opportunity to wash off the dust from Bamaga Road.

We play in the water and sit under the waterfalls long enough to bring our body temperatures down. I could have stayed there for the rest of the day, but the allure of a cold tinnie motivates me to continue. We also have a deadline to make it to the Jardine Ferry before it closes. We are all looking forward to making our camp at the famous Punsand Bay camping ground.

The northern bypass starts as a recently-graded road but quickly becomes the most horrendous collection of speed bumps on the trip. Trying to keep up some speed to float across the corrugations is a constant battle. The road is about sixty metres wide, and tall, dark green eucalyptus forests frame the bright, ochre-coloured road.

Ahead are clouds of blue-grey smoke, which drift like fog across the road, cutting sunlight and reducing visibility. Is it a bushfire? Am I was riding into a blazing inferno or is it some locals burning off? The corrugations are deeper and harder than any I have yet ridden across, the tall trees prevent any breeze, and the choking smoke are all conspiring to lift my anxiety levels. It seems to take forever, but eventually, I make it to the Jardine Ferry.

As usual, the others are waiting for me. Shayla is lying on the concrete to try to cool off, Quentin and Rob are in the shade of the ferry office, and Nick and Flemming are sitting under the shade of a barbeque table near the public toilets. I quickly enter the small office at Jardine River Park and purchase my ticket for the ferry. It costs fifty dollars for each bike, double that for cars, and more for vehicles towing trailers.

When I first see the river, I'm surprised it's not bigger. All the stories I've heard of drowned four-wheel drives in the river didn't fit the small creek we are about to cross. I was anticipating it would be about the same size as the Daintree River. Realistically, if they had built the ferry four metres longer, it wouldn't need to move; lower the gates, and everyone could drive over like a floating bridge.

The Jardine Ferry is as much a part of the experience of riding to Cape York as are the termite mounds; it's a creaking, rusty floating platform. You could see the river between the board on the floor; as the ferry moved, it groaned and twisted. I get off Emu to take some photos and, as I turn around, the ferry twisted slightly.

Emu falls over. Having opened my tank bag to take out my camera, I was lucky the rest of the contents didn't end up in the mouth of a crocodile. Rob was the first to reach Emu and quickly returned him to an upright position with only minor scratches on his engine protection bars.

The further north you go, the worse the Bamaga Road becomes. When I ask the guy at the ferry office what the road from Jardine to Bamaga was like, he just laughs, "It's almost as good as the last forty kilometres," he replied with a cheerful grin. I'm hoping it's a good sign, but am in for some disappointment. Roads in India that hang off cliffs and long, flat, sandy sections of roads in Africa are better maintained than the road from Jardine to Bamaga.

Nothing we could do, of course, except ride it. . The final forty kilometres of the Bamaga Road are, without a doubt, the hardest stretch of road so far. The vibrations are so bad that I have to stop to remove my GPS because I am concerned about losing the whole panel. My KLR dash broke, and the bolts are about to fall out. I pull out my multi-tool and tightened as many as I can and use cable ties on the dash, that will have to do until I get to camp.

The corrugations are huge, and the road itself is a constant wave. It is like corrugations on corrugations. It's hot and it's late in the day. Looking up the road, I couldn't see an end to this torturous road.

I have ridden over bone-jarring terrain all day, and I didn't want to get back on the bike. But I resolved to keep going until the end. At times like these, you know the only way to fix your immediate situation is to keep going. I jump on the pegs and take off as fast as I could. There comes a time when you must dig deep into your inner strength, and this is one of those times.

Fifteen kilometres on, I catch up with my compatriots who have decided to take a deter road into Bamaga via the airport. It is a small dirt road that went up into the hills. I look back down the main Bamaga Road as it disappears towards the town; it's a long line of deep corrugations. It's horrendously bad; even deep sand would have been better as tricky as riding in deep sand is, at least it would be smooth.

The rainforest and scrub in the hills makes a welcome change from the dry beach scrub of the Bamaga road. It is cooler, and there are fewer corrugations. Eventually, the road came to a tee intersection, and we are back on the tar. We form into a riding group and coast to the Bamaga BP station. We have made it. We fill up with fuel, buy more water bottles and prepare for the final dirt section.

Punsand Bay is about twenty five kilometres north of Bamaga and slightly west of Cape York. I'm exhausted, and the only thing driving me is the thought of cold beer at the famous "Corrugation Bar." But it requires us to hit the dirt once again, and for some time, the corrugations are almost as bad as the Bamaga Road.

Luckily, these speed bumps don't last long, and we are winding through rainforest and beachside scrub again. There is also a slight but deep creek crossing to add to the fun and wash some red dirt from the wheels and engine.

We come to the small shop called the Crocodile Tent and turn left toward Punsand Bay. We are close to the tip. Riding straight would have taken us there. But that would have to wait until tomorrow. We just wanted to get to a campsite, set up our tents, take off our riding gear, and sit at the bar overlooking the Endeavour Strait and Punsand Bay.

We will stay here for a couple of nights before heading back. Tonight, we will have one more beer and maybe a red wine.

I can now understand the allure of this road. It's a road less travelled but one that is travelled by those who seek adventure. There's a kind of brotherhood at this campground, with everybody who has made it to the top celebrating at the aptly named "Corrugation Bar."

But I have a nagging anxiety that I would have to ride the corrugations back down the PDR in a couple of days. Is there an easier way? Maybe I could put the bike on the supply ship that runs up the coast from Cairns? Nick hands me a beer, and that thought disappears.

'Cheers, mate,' I said, "We're almost there." We clanked bottles and skulled the beers, "One more?" I said when both bottles were empty, "Why not!".

Chapter 26
The Northern Tip of the Australian Continent

"You don't have to be a fantastic hero to do certain things - to compete. You can be just an ordinary chap, sufficiently motivated to reach challenging goals."

– Edmund Hillary

Many people have bucket lists that include the journey to the tip of Australia. Standing at the northernmost point of the Australian continent, one feels a profound sense of accomplishment.

A week ago, the journey to the tip seemed like a big goal. Like all good journeys, it starts with the first step and the determination to continue.

I could see an island as I looked across the small gap of fast-flowing water, with its whirlpools and deep azure water. Then another, and I can't help wondering what's on those islands. This is the true essence of an explorer: Where to next?

We arrived at the Punsand Bay Resort on the western side of Cape York last night. At the camping ground, we set up our tents as a group before going to the bar for a much-needed beer and a bite to eat. The resort consists of a combination of tent sites and glamping accommodation.

The entire front of the resort is a beach that looks out to the Arafura Sea; it is a fantastic view over the tranquil water that changes colour as the sun goes down. When making our way to the tables with our drinks, the sea is a translucent purple.

We have a great night which kicked off sitting around the pool drinking icy-cold, albeit expensive, beer. When it comes time for dinner, some of the others have beautifully-presented mackerel meals. I have a large meat lover's pizza. It is a sublime experience not wearing shoes or boots for the first time in four days.

In the morning, we are in no hurry, preferring to have a leisurely breakfast and the standard two cups of coffee. I prepped myself for the ride to the tip. At this stage on our journey, I have run out of clean clothes. I spend the early part of the morning washing all my shirts. Rob strung a line, and we all used it to dry our washing.

The only shirt that is dry and clean is an old rag full of holes that I intended to use to clean my chain. I throw it under my armour and ride to the tip in rags. We strip the touring luggage from the bikes to make them more responsive and ride back through the beach scrub, along the dusty road, through the small creek crossing which became deeper overnight, and back to the Croc Tent.

At the Croc Tent, we turned left and ride the fifteen kilometres to the northern tip of the Australian continent.

I don't know what to expect on the final road to the tip; I guess more of the same. But after two minutes of riding, I come across the most stunning rainforest; the road turns into a track with tight turns, red clay soil and significant drop-offs. On a motorbike, it's great fun, and my attitude is more kid-like, pushing the bike into corners, pulling a wheely coming over small bumps, and generally riding without a care. It would be a slow, bumpy trip in a car.

Eventually, the road widens out, allowing for a bit more speed. I follow Rob, who is power sliding at every corner; I follow suit, and we are back on our dirt bikes as kids.

As I ride to the car park, I pass the Panjinka Wilderness Lodge which is about four hundred metres from the end of Cape York Road. It was established by the company Bush Pilots Airline in 1989 for one million, two hundred thousand dollars. QANTAS acquired it, but it was sold several times throughout its short history. Today, it's an abandoned relic of the past, with broken shutters and tilting verandas belying its glory days of parties, dancing, and fine dining.

The final nail in the coffin was a generator fire, which prevented the site from pumping water. It was closed in 2002. In its day, it was the only five-star resort in the Cape. It's a shame that a simple generator issue could have prevented such an amazing place from thriving. At a time when roads were almost non-existent, the journey to the tip would have been by plane and only available to wealthy tourists.

In November 2019, the land and resort were handed over to the Gudang/Yadhaykenu people. There were great expectations that it would be restored and turned into a cultural tourism facility and camping site by early 2020. This development would be an amazing asset to the Gudang and Yadhaykenu people. However, from the looks of it, the refurbishment has yet to begin.

The sun is burning as we peeled off most of our riding gear. The humidity is about eighty per cent; and there is no breeze in the car parking area. I prepare myself for the nine-hundred-metre walk over Pajinka Hill. It is the final leg of my quest to the northern tip of Australia.

I wear my raggedy old shirt, body armour jacket, riding pants, and boots. I quickly become hot and sweaty, and each step feels like climbing a big mountain. The only one who had thought about what she would wear for the auspicious occasion was Shayla who dressed appropriately in active wear.

Where she stored all her clothes on her bike is still a mystery. If we had given out prizes, she would have won the best-dressed competition. I, on the other hand, would have won the worst-dressed prize.

Once at the top, I can see the path down to the tip. The sea breeze is kicking in and keeping me cool. As I walk over the hill, I see a breathtaking vista below. In front are York Island and Eborac Island, with its lighthouse.

To the left, two sailing catamarans are moored in Punsand Bay. Further on, we see the Bay and Peak Points, and what we think is the famous Possession Island, which is peeking out above the mainland. Looking beyond the islands is the Torres Islands and the Arafura Sea.

The significance of Possession Island is that Captain Cook planted the Union Jack and declared the land for England, much to the bewilderment of the local Aboriginal people standing watching. The water is a stunning azure, with patches of deep blue and what look like small reefs dotted randomly around just under the water.

The journey to the tip is within my grasp! I make my way down to the point. The deep blue-green water of the channel between the Australian continent and York Island is incredibly inviting, but you have to risk sharks, crocodiles and marine stingers to take a dip here, not to mention the rip. As I get closer, I can see the current running through the gap between the mainland and Eborac Island.

It is fast-flowing and turbulent; now and then, a whirlpool forms, grows, and then collapses on itself. People are standing on the point fishing. What sacrilege is this? Didn't they know this is Holy Ground?

Then I wondered what the Aboriginal people fishing from this point would have thought as they watched a giant sailing ship meander through the passage. Would they have known they were standing on the northern point of what would become the Australian continent? Or was it simply another great fishing spot?

I did it! I made it to the northernmost tip of the Australian continent. It is an enlightening moment, but I have to wait my turn to get in front of the sign. There are about twenty people around us.

Everyone is very friendly, and they ask if they could take our photos and we ask them if we could take theirs. We take individual and group photos to ensure we can post pictures of ourselves all over social media.

I talk with a couple about their experiences. When I ask them how far they have sailed, they look at me quizzically, "How do you know we sailed here?" they asked.

I replied, "It's obvious, you're the only people here with clean clothes". "And you're wearing white shorts and boat shoes."

We talk about sailing and motorcycle adventures. Although we are miles apart culturally, as adventurers, we have so much in common. They are waiting for the winds to change so they can sail directly south and avoid constant tacking. These winds will soon change, as the monsoon season begins. They plan to sail back down the east coast of Australia to their home on the Sunshine Coast. They aren't in any hurry.

We take turns getting in front of the famous sign that states, "You are standing on the northernmost point of the Australian continent." It is a surreal Moment; as far as moments go. There is no doubt this one will stand above all the others I've encountered on my travels. I have ridden almost twenty thousand kilometres around Queensland. I have travelled from the bottom of Queensland to the very top of Australia.

I sit silently, looking out over the deep blue waters of the Endeavour Passage, and contemplate how lucky I am to be sitting here and how, two years ago, this would have been another unobtainable dream. After twenty minutes, I get up, turn and head back to the car park. I consumed my remaining water, helped push Nick's bike, and returned to the Croc tent to get the obligatory T-shirt to prove I had been there.

The Croc Tent sits at the corner of the Bamaga, Punsand Bay and the track to the tip. It's a tent with a vast collection of shirts, mugs, stubbie coolers and fridge magnets. There are shirts for all tastes and budgets with the one important message: "You made it to the top of Australia." As we arrive, a family was leaving, having just been fitted out with matching shirts.

I bought a shirt to replace the rag I was wearing, one that said "I made it to the tip on a motorbike," and a singlet that simply said "Cape York." As I was walking back to my bike, I detect the unmistakable smell of coolant. I try to dismiss the smell, but as I get closer, I see water dripping down the front of the radiator. There was no doubt I had a radiator leak.

Of all the places to have a leaky radiator! I'm in one of the remotest parts of Australia on a dirt track many miles from the nearest town. At these times, all the possible solutions go through your mind within the first five minutes. How can I get the bike home? Can I get home? What will it cost to get the bike on the ferry to Cairns? How do I get it to the ferry? Can I get someone here to help, or must I fly back by charter flight?

I consider all the possible solutions except the one that really matters: how do I plug the leak? Nick, Shayla, and Quentin come up, and I explain the problem. There is only one solution: get a radiator 'Stop-Leak Fluid', and plug the hole. Why didn't I think of that? Actually, I did, but I dismissed it in favour of more elaborate solutions.

The Croc Tent people are helpful and give me water to fill the radiator. With the solution in hand, I fill the tank and set off for Bamaga. Finding the shop that sells radiator goo takes some time. I wait for Emu to cool down, open the cap, start the engine and fill the tank with about a third of the bottle. Emu hasn't lost much water, which is good news. Once I run the engine, I top it up with water and ride back to Punsand Bay.

Nobody has much faith in the solution, but it is all we can do now. If it holds great, if not, we will have to think of an alternative. We have averted disaster for now, so I shower and put on one of my new shirts. I feel clean and respectable again. We order beer and put our feet up to watch the sun setting on a fabulous day.

A little while later, Shayla and her mum (via the Wi-Fi connection) decide to buy dinner for everyone as a celebration. We share a mackerel pizza; I have a couple of glasses of red wine and sit back again to watch the sunset. Could the day have ended any better?

It isn't long before we all wander off to bed. Tomorrow, we start our journey home via the Lion's Den Hotel, another North Queensland icon.

Chapter 27
The Journey Home

He who returns from a journey is not the same as he who left. – Chinese Proverb

It's five in the morning, and the journey home has begun. I've been awake, lying on my mat, listening to the wind in the trees. It's time to pack up. I'm fully packed within half an hour except for my cooking gear. I sit down to enjoy a couple of cups of coffee. I can hear the others starting to stir. Quentin is also beginning to pack; we're hoping for an early start this morning and will do most of our riding before the day's heat hits us.

The journey to the tip is only half the story. We now have to start our journey home. With one of the DRZs not starting and the KLR with a radiator leak, the journey home is likely to be dramatic. We are hoping everything will hang together and keep working. We have over eight hundred kilometres to ride over the next two days and must monitor both bikes closely. Our return journey will be difficult, with corrugated bulldust and temperatures over thirty-five degrees Celsius.

As the sun rises, I walk down to the beach for the last time. It's a good time to take photos; the light is harmonious and soft. The bar and swimming pool areas are devoid of people and unusually quiet. It's funny how a place takes on a different feeling when no one is around.

Luckily, the bar staff has left out a one-hundred-litre container of drinking water which I can use to fill my bladders and bottles. At six dollars for a three hundred-ml plastic bottle, I would be paying more for water than fuel.

Nick, Shayla, and I leave first. On the way, we stop at the Croc Tent for Nick to get another T-shirt. We continue to Bamaga, where we fuelled up. The next fuel station after that is Bramwell Junction Roadhouse two hundred kilometres away which is our destination for the day.

There's no problem with fuel; we all have over three hundred and fifty kilometres of range in the tanks. But we've been riding around for the past few days, and I have a rule: do not leave a significant town without filling up. I definitely don't want to run out of fuel on the journey home.

I fill Emu's tank and sit on the small wall in front of the station, eating a toasted sandwich and chugging down an energy drink, waiting for the others to arrive. It's going to be a long day; I need as much energy as possible. Knowing what the road was like, I had to get myself prepared for the constant corrugations and dry, dusty road.

Soon, the others arrive. While they fill up, I check my radiator's water levels—all good so far. We are all anxious to get on with our journey home. It is early, so we kept an eye out for kangaroos.

Bluetooth communication devices are great, provided you're not too far away from each other. We are spread out over about five kilometres as we ride through the rainforest and bush areas to join the Bamaga Road. I can barely hear what the others are saying. From what I can hear, it sounds like someone hit a roo. This is our worst fear: one of our riders is down and needs an evacuation.

I have pulled up, as had Rob and Shayla when we hear Nick's voice clear over the comms, "I've just hit a fucking roo, but I'm still going". It appears a small wallaby shot out of the bush. With no way of missing it, Nick braced for the impact and hit it straight on.

There's not much else you can do; it takes strength of character to know you're about to hit something, and you have to let it happen. If Nick had swerved hard to try and avoid the wallaby, he might have lost control of his bike on the loose gravel road. But by sitting back and bracing the motorcycle, he could keep control and keep moving forward.

Often, the correct action is counterintuitive, like riding sand. When the wheel digs in, you want to hit the brakes. This is a recipe for disaster; the correct technique is to accelerate and bring your weight back. When you hit a roo, brace for impact, stay upright for as long as possible and try and find a clear space to land.

As the animal went under the front of Nick's bike, it hit his boot hard enough to cause some bruising to his ankle. Nick was still moving, and the bike responded appropriately. The roo had taken off but would have been sore.

It's not until Nick gets back on the tar the next day that the extent of the bike's damage became evident. The incident put a small dent in the front wheel and, while riding dirt, Nick didn't notice the vibration, but once on the tar, it became apparent.

It wasn't long before we arrive at Jardine Ferry; it didn't seem as long to return as it did to get there. I guess this is the nature of the journey home; some of the roads are familiar. My temperature gauge starts to climb as I get closer to the ferry. This indicates the radiator is leaking again, so I have to stop and add water.

Once at the ferry, I wait for the radiator to cool down enough to remove the cap. Sure enough, the water level has fallen. I add the last of my stop-leak goo and fill the radiator as the bike motor gurgled all the air out of the system. After replacing the cap, there is no sign of water leaking.

As soon as we hit the road, we steel ourselves for the next forty kilometres. We are keen to get this stretch behind us as fast as possible. In my mind, this represents the worst of the Bamaga Road, and from then on, the road is just bad, not really bad.

I grit my teeth and head south through the torturous bulldust and corrugations. Finally, we arrive at the Fruit Bat Falls entrance and the southern entry to the northern section of the OTT. Rob and Shayla are waiting at the beginning. Flemming has taken off early.

The track to Elliot Falls is all deep sand. The only way to ride this track is fast; I stand up, sit back on my top bag and keep the bike in third gear. This gives me a pretty good rev range and allows enough torque to drive out if I get into trouble, but not so fast that I lose control.

Rob rides past me about halfway, so I decide to speed up to follow his line; I move forward slightly as I went to click up a gear. But instead of clicking up, I accidentally went down. Emu goes into panic mode; I'm sure I could hear him say something like, "What the fuck are you doing?" or maybe that was me; it was all a bit confusing.

Everything happened at the same time. The front wheel drops and is buried in the soft sand, and I lose all control of the bike's direction. The front wheel pulls me from side to side as I wrestle with the handlebars to maintain control. I want to hit the brakes and stop, but I know if I do that, I will be high-siding it over the handlebars into the trees and rocks on the side of the track.

I do what all my instincts told me not to do; I twist the throttle and accelerate, pulling back on the handlebars, and leaning as far back as possible. Once I have the front wheel straight and rising, I go up a gear and am on top of the sand again. Luckily, I come across Canal Creek and can stop and take some deep breaths with Emu secure on the hard dirt above the creek.

Canal Creek has a steep rocky entry with deep wheel trenches, which is ideal for bikes; although fully loaded, you still need to find the correct line as it has a steep entry. There are a couple of camper vans on the left side of the creek, free camping, which looks like a perfect place to camp.

Although the causeway has an inch or two of water, it is easily crossed. However, the climb out is a steep, potholed hill, after which it is back onto the sand. This would be a lot more difficult to cross when deeper water flows in it.

The sand doesn't last long and we are soon entering Jardine National Park and Elliot Twin Falls car park. We assemble and stripped out of our riding gear before following the boardwalk down to the Falls. I am glad to have my knee braces on during my sand entanglement, but they have been rubbing on the top of my knee for some time which is quite painful.

For long distances, these braces are uncomfortable. I am relieved to take them off and get my knees into the cool, refreshing water. We sat in the water, climbed the rock ledges and jumped back into the water again. A series of smaller waterfalls and a safe area suitable for families and children is located on the downriver side.

Elliot Twin Falls has several different places to swim and is equally spectacular as Fruit Bat Falls. The river is wide at the top and resembles a deep frying pan before cascading over a narrow rock ledge about five metres high. From there, it spreads out slightly and rushes down into an open, narrow gorge. The water has a translucent green glow. The waterfalls are generally free of crocodiles; the rapids and sheer rock faces of the falls prevent crocs from coming upstream.

You can't come to the Cape and not see these magnificent natural features. We would have liked to look around this area and camp the night, but we still have one hundred and twenty kilometres of riding in front of us today.

I make my way back up the boardwalk, through the vegetation to the car park, and then back onto the northern section of the OTT. The ride back was nowhere near as eventful as the ride in. After my near-death experience, I decide to apply the slower, and probably less safe, sand riding technique of dragging my feet for the next eleven kilometres, much to the bewilderment of my travelling companions who race past me.

The incident earlier with the sand makes me start to wonder about the issues Emu and I were having with suspension geometry. Something is not quite right about how he is performing, and I couldn't put my finger on it. The back end is soft. Every time I apply power, rather than digging in, he twists from side to side, causing the front wheel to wobble and lift. It is an exaggeration of my previous issues along the bulldust-laden roads.

We all make it to the exit except Flemming. No one has seen him since we pulled up at the Fruit Bat Falls entrance. He has taken off in the lead, and we haven't seen him again. We suspect he went to Fruit Bat Falls rather than Elliot. Quentin decides to go and find him while the rest of us continue on our way.

It wasn't long before Quentin and Flemming pass me. I am keeping an eye on the temperature gauge and struggling to keep the front wheel in the right line. If I couldn't figure out what's wrong with Emu, the rest of the journey home will be painful.

I notice the temperature gauge climbing again about ten kilometres out of Bramwell Junction. It is a straight, good section of road, but when I stop, I can feel the heat—it was like opening an oven. I pull up and remove the radiator cap. The sun is well and truly burning, and there is no airflow on the road.

The water level is so low I couldn't see it, so I fill the tank with the remaining water. I keep the engine running to ensure cold water didn't enter the engine and cause thermal cracking. Then, I replace the cap and head towards the roadhouse. I'm sure it isn't far, and no sooner do I have this thought than the dirt changes to tar. I ride over the hill to see the roadhouse below.

When I arrive at the Bramwell Junction Roadhouse, I immediately went to the fuel bowser to fill up, ready for the next day. Quentin had become concerned about my delayed arrival. He had been reassured that I was alright by a guy in a Landcruiser who passed me while I was filling Emu's radiator tank.

He decides we need to take drastic action to fix my radiator issue, or we wouldn't meet our travel goals for our journey home tomorrow. One of the people at the roadhouse has a bit of radiator putty while the station owner came out with a bottle of radiator stop-leak goo.

He claims it will fix a D9 bulldozer radiator. How could I not buy a bottle? At twenty dollars, it's a bargain. However, I couldn't help feeling he was a bit of a snake oil salesman. Could it do what the other goo could not do?

As I talked to the guy, Quentin pulled the radiator off Emu and brought it to the roadhouse. The solution was multifaceted: First, cut the fins away from the tube at the offending site. Second, apply liberal amounts of radiator putty to the affected area and beyond. Third, pinch the tubes near the hole at the top and bottom to reduce pressure in the offending area. Fourth, add old mate's radiator goo to the system and hope for the best.

Within no time, the repairs have been made, and all that is left is for me to run the engine hot for about twenty minutes to enable the goo to circulate and do its thing. I jump on Emu, and we race up and down the five kilometres of tar, reaching speeds up to one hundred thirty kilometres per hour.

After twenty minutes, there are no signs of leaks, and the engine has maintained a constant low temperature. It was time for a cold beer.

As we discuss the day's events and our plans for tomorrow, I mention to Nick how Emu has been behaving in the sand and the problem of the back wheel sliding around. Between Nick, Quentin, and Flemming, there's not much they don't know about bikes and their setup.

As Emu has a top-of-the-range "Moab" suspension system front and back, Nick believes it is more likely an adjustment setting on the back spring. Nick then adjusts Emu's rear suspension by about three notches to take up more of the free travel. This would help engage the rear shock sooner and increase the pressure on the back wheel.

While packing my kit, I notice I am packing my tools on the exhaust side, which makes them heavier than the opposite side. Considering the pannier on the right side of the bike is stepped further out to accommodate the exhaust, this would create a difference in weight distribution.

I also want to reduce the weight in the top bag. To balance the weight, I transfer the tent and some tools to the left pannier and move some lighter material to the top bag. I hope I now have a balanced bike.

That night, we have a banquet of all the leftover dried meals. Shayla cooks while I boil water in my jetfoil for the packaged meals. What is not eaten is discarded into the rubbish bins, which makes our bikes much lighter and easier to pack.

We decide that we would attempt to make the journey to the famous Lion's Den hotel the next day; a distance of approximately six hundred kilometres, with a substantial part of that on dirt, bulldust and corrugations. Hopefully, the bikes would hold together.

A number of our group have only heard about the famous pub but have not been there. We pack up as the sun was starting to rise and leave at seven in the morning. We are particularly concerned about roos, but as the roads are wide and the traffic non-existent, the risk is pretty low.

As soon as I hit the dirt, I could feel the difference in Emu's performance; his rear end is no longer unstable, and the front is lighter. As I increased speed, I feel the front wheel keep its line, and the bike generally is quite comfortable. This makes me look forward to the trail and find the best lines.

It's as if I am riding a different bike. I cruise comfortably between ninety-five and one hundred kilometres per hour on the open straights; I trail brake through the corners and then accelerate again.

Trail braking involves applying pressure to the back brake to control the rear wheel as you corner. This enables you to release the brake as you accelerate, keeping the back shock absorbers engaged throughout the curve and driving the bike in the direction you choose when you come out of the corner.

For quite a while, I ride just behind Flemming until the dust becomes too much. At that point, I drop back further but am able to keep him in sight. When it comes to the tar-sealed roads, I catch up again, only to drop back with the dust.

We arrive at Archer River Roadhouse in no time and stop to wait for the others. Quentin comments over the intercom that he has just passed a slow-moving truck and that we should continue quickly. I tell Rob, and we hit the road. It isn't long before we come across another slow-moving truck that reduces the visibility to zero.

Rob gets past, and Flemming follows, disappearing into the dust. I sit back for some time until, to my surprise, the truck driver pulls up so I can pass.

As soon as I hit the tar again, I do what the KLR does well: I speed up to a little over highway speed. It wasn't long before I pull into Coen. Rob has started to fill his tank, so I couldn't have been too far behind.

Rob and I are standing outside the Coen store, waiting for the others to arrive, when a luxury off-road tour bus pulls up. Four well-dressed, middle-aged women, with gold and diamonds, step out of the bus. One lady wearing a fashionable linen dress with a black leather belt approaches me and asks if she and her friends could take a photo with us.

We agree, and they start taking selfies with one between each of us. They walk over, take pictures of the bikes, and ask if we could stand by the bikes with each of them.

Now, I'm not saying that Rob and I exude a high level of mature male charisma, but clearly these chicks are in awe of our rugged manly looks and careless disregard for our safety. Maybe a new career as a macho male model was worth considering?

We stop at the Hann River Roadhouse to regather before hitting the trail again. Quentin is racing to overtake a truck that passed him before it gets to the next section of dirt. While he gets past, Rob and I are trapped. The small section of dirt that caused us some concern on the way up came and went quickly without concern this time. We are able to overtake the truck as it starts to climb one of the hills.

We pass through Laura quickly and continue on. At about ten kilometres before the Lakeland Roadhouse, I feel Emu stutter and begin to slow down. I look at my temperature gauge, Emu is within the cool limits, and then at my trip metre.

According to my calculations, I should have at least another fifty kilometres before the reserve. I fumble with my fuel valve and finally manage to turn it to reserve. Emu kicks back into life, and I get back up to speed.

The day is almost over, with only fifty kilometres until we reach the famous Lion's Den Hotel. Having ridden one of the longest days of our journey, we are about to achieve a significant event in adventure riding. The temperature has started to drop as the day begins to wane, and the ride up Mulligan's Highway is a welcome relief from the eight days of hard riding.

This is our journey home, but not the end of our adventure. I've been to The Lion's Den Hotel before during my Daintree adventure, but this time I'm with fellow riders on a public holiday. Luckily, the pub was going off, and there is live music, beer and pizzas.

Chapter 28
The Lion's Den Hotel

The Lion's Den Hotel is a classic Australian outback pub; in essence, it's a tin shack. At the front is an old hitching post, and a large male lion statue protects the front entry. Out the side, a band is playing blues music on the deck, and as I walk up to the pub, I can hear the sounds of people talking, glasses clinking, and kids playing.

We manage to get there during the busiest time of the year, the Queen's Birthday weekend. The grounds are packed. Along with those who have just completed the Creb Track, a number of bike groups are heading to the tip. They are starting their adventure, while we are almost at the end of ours.

We meet up with Ellyse O'Connor, part owner of Ellwood Motorcycle Adventures, and her trail lead, Rex. They have an excellent setup and have just led a group up the Creb Track. They are kicking back at the Lion's Den before going to Cooktown, then through Lakeland National Park via Old Laura. From there, they will be heading north to the Old Telegraph Track.

They are an awesome bunch of people and, as fellow adventure bikers, they are very interested in our experiences. There's an instant camaraderie between bikers, especially adventure riders. It's like you've found your family.

They are friendly towards us, giving us inside information about the various places we have visited but not realised their significance. We chat about all things motorcycle, and they tell us a lot about their different experiences of the Cape.

Ellyse is particularly impressed with Shayla, who is possibly one of the youngest riders to do the Cape ride unsupported. She mentions that they hold women-only riding events and are planning a run across the Simpson Desert. She suggests that Shayla consider joining them. It's great that women in this industry are trying to build up the ranks of female adventure riders and are prepared to mentor younger riders.

Once we find our campsite and set up our tents, it's time to wash off the red dust and get a drink at the bar. We settle down to talk about our trip and other planned activities as we eat lots of garlic bread and pizza. We kick back and listen to live music until late in the evening (at least nine o'clock).

We decide to take our time leaving the next day. Rob and Flemming are riding into Cooktown to look around. I am intending to drain my radiator to clear out the goo circulating in the engine but change my mind when one of the guys from Ellwood comes over to talk to me about the KLRs.

He has had the same problem. But when he drained the bike, he damaged the water pump gasket and had to get the motorcycle taken out on a trailer. He suggests that I leave it until I am home and closer to a Kawasaki dealer. We talk a lot about KLRs; he wants to know how my bike performed on the trip up. We share stories until it is time for him to get on the road.

While waiting for Rob and Flemming to return, I have a coffee at the bar and began talking with the owner. The story of the hotel's name is painted on the walls. It goes like this: Now Daniel had two vices: beer and women.

- The first panel at the counter of Daniel's Diner shows Daniel pushing his cart of tin ore from the mine across the road to the hotel.
- The second panel which is around the corner shows him taking it straight to Sheila's Shack, but for what reason, we are not sure.
- After spending some time with Sheila, Daniel decides to go to the hotel bar for a beer. If you look closely at the swing doors, you will see that Daniel has forgotten to tuck something in. Again, we can only assume what Sheila and Daniel got up to.
- In the final panel, Daniel's pants are on backwards, which is different from when he pushed the tin ore to Sheila's Shack.

From the above narrative, I can only assume Sheila was a tin ore merchant and a seamstress. It makes perfect sense.

It wasn't long before Rob and Flemming turn up, and we are ready to begin the last stage of our Cape York Adventure. This is indeed the journey home. But before we hit the main highway, we have to ride the very steep Bloomfield Track and cross the infamous Emmagen Creek.

The ride to Wujal Wujal is exhilarating. It features sweeping corners and long straights with cool tropical vegetation. It is early morning, and the sun is rising over the trees. The air is cool but moist. While there seems to be less traffic on the road, that is until we started to climb up into the Daintree. We then realise how busy the roads were this weekend.

What would typically be a tranquil ride through dense rainforest became a ride through dust clouds with four-wheel drives and camper trailers racing to get up the steep concrete inclines. It is the most dangerous part of our adventure; at times, coming down the steep concrete road with almost zero visibility, I would come across the driver of a four-wheel vehicle racing to get up towards us.

We communicate via the headsets, and at times, I pull over until the racing vehicle had made it up the steep incline. We are all greatly relieved when we reach Emmagen Creek and Cape Tribulation.

The experienced riders have no problem crossing the creek. Shayla is behind me, following my line, when, without warning, she stalls. Being a bit small to put both feet down, she precariously balances the bike on one leg. I park my bike on the side of the creek and race back to help. Luckily, the water hasn't reached the air intake, and a major dewatering is averted.

We assemble at Cape Tribulation township, then carry on to the famous ice cream shop, riding in loose formation over bridges of small crystal clear creeks and dense rainforests. Eventually, we make it to the Daintree Ferry. We take lots of photos of the bikes and our group.

This is the end of our adventure; not long after exiting the ferry, we arrive in Mossman. I continue south through Cairns and stay the night at a motel in Innisfail, while the rest would go up to Mount Molloy and back to Atherton.

Seeing my friends pull out from the Mossman Petrol station and ride off into the sunset is sad. This trip is one of the most incredible motorcycle adventures I have experienced. I will never forget it as a fantastic adventure with great people.

Getting to the tip and back is a monumental effort, being eight days of constant riding. There is still so much more to explore on the Cape; I think we'll come back, possibly on lighter bikes with support vehicles, so we can explore the OTT and some of the tracks up at the tip.

Chapter 29
A New Beginning

This is the end of my great adventure around Queensland. At over twenty thousand kilometres, I have barely scratched the surface of adventure motorcycle riding in Australia. I have travelled lonely roads and long dusty highways and managed to stay alive, despite suicidal kangaroos on lonely outback roads and stressed-out commuters in Queensland's biggest city, Brisbane.

Looking back, I often wonder if I would do it all again. The answer is a resounding 'Yes!' but I wouldn't do it the same way. I would take longer, stay at some fantastic beaches I've discovered, soak up the tropical environments, and engage more with locals.

I have learnt and seen so much that I am a changed person. I have a renewed zest for life and a longing for a life of adventure, whatever that might mean. The only question I have now is: where to go next?

I no longer worry about the future or sitting at a desk for the rest of my life, letting life pass me by. Am I on the path to enlightenment? Maybe. That path involves, at least sometimes, riding a motorbike and seeking out the wonder in this world in a way that only riding a bike can provide.

I'm a much better rider than two years ago; I'm not anxious about getting on my bike and taking off on an adventure. I'm not concerned about riding in the mud or sand because I know how to. I also know how to read the road or track, so I can ride fast when I need to or slow down when I have to. I have learnt to pack light, fix my bike when it breaks, and that all problems can be fixed with a little patience.

Chapter 30
What Have I Learnt?

Do I consider myself an experienced adventure rider? Not really. I can hold my own with other riders in most situations. I don't think I will ever be a fast rider, but I can handle single track, mud and sand now without freaking out. There are four main things I have learned from a 20,000-kilometre ride around Queensland and life on the road as a biker:

One
The first time you put the bike into gear to leave on a trip, you feel an overwhelming desire to turn it off. You think you are leaving your family and being selfish, and don't think you can or should be doing this.

I learnt that an adventure makes you a better person, that you come back with knowledge to share and that your outlook on life is different. The proverb that the person who goes on an adventure is not the same person who returns is very true.

As soon as you hit the road and turn into the first roundabout, when home is no longer in the mirror, the adventure begins. You will learn that you have to rely on yourself and your bike. This is the beginning of a great adventure, your adventure.

Two
When planning this great adventure, I packed what I felt I needed and not what I actually needed. My insecurities had me take everything I could think of to counter any eventuality on the road. I realised I didn't need all that gear as I rode.

For example, outback pubs don't care what you wear, and thongs, stubbies, and tee shirts are considered smart casual. So, a biker shirt, boots and jeans are almost overdressing; places that require you to dress up aren't places you will frequent as an adventure rider.

Other examples are tools; a complete socket set would be great, but it's excess weight. Work out what sockets you need for your bike and only take those. A solar panel is essential when sitting for weeks in the outback sun, but it's pointless on a motorbike tour. Install a USB charger on your bike or pull it up at a campground and use the power in the camp kitchen. I have done this many times.

I took a twenty-thousand milliamp battery as a backup and would probably do this again. My tool collection was pretty standard but also included a small multimeter, chain brake, spare link, gas-powered soldering iron (for radiator leaks), tubes, a small 12-volt air compressor, tyre levers, and talc for helping get the tyre back on the rim.

Your bike can easily hold everything if you are careful about what you need to survive. What isn't packed can be purchased with a credit card on the way.

Three

To keep the costs down while travelling, I engaged in quite a bit of wild camping; that's always a great idea. But stories of tourists being harassed, killed or kidnapped keep coming back into your mind. Will I be safe? What if my bike gets stolen? What if someone attacks me?

Camping in the wild is not dangerous, provided you take some precautions. Learn to read the signs, look for secure places to camp and don't harm yourself. Always have an escape plan and ensure you lock away your valuables and secure your bike. And if you are concerned, do what my friend Peter does: pack early as the sun comes up and don't put up your tent until it is almost dark—camp in an area where trees or walls protect you and keep your bike hidden.

I always put a camo cover over Emu and a brake lock. Wild camping is not accepted in most urban areas, and many councils frown on the practice. So if wild camping in these areas, be extra careful to conceal your camp; you could be fined if found.

I have been travelling around Queensland on Emu for two years, and in the 45 years before that, I car camped in parts of Australia and New Zealand. Once in New Zealand, I backed the car into a car sales yard and slept in it. I have never been harassed while wild camping.

Four

Solo riding in Australia can be a lonely experience. There are long distances and isolated communities, and you're far from your regular support network.

I learnt to trust my judgement, make decisions based on facts, not emotions, and ensure my bike and I had the maintenance and resources needed to fix any problems.

If you're going west into the outback, take plenty of water and make sure someone knows where you're going, even if that is the local police officer in the community you're starting your journey in. I carry a Personal Locator Beacon (PLB) attached to my backpack. If I'm in a life-threatening situation, I will not hesitate to call for help.

You can be alone and not be lonely; it's how you look at the world. I know many people in the middle of cities who feel lonely. In Australia, there are always people to talk with and places you can go to take your mind off the loneliness. Someone will always stop and help you. It's the Australian way.

Chapter 31
The End of the Beginning

I started this adventure because I felt that life was drifting by and, if I didn't stop and look around, I would grow too old to realise my dreams. I started as a novice adventure rider but, through the wisdom of others and my desire to be better, I have learnt to ride in almost any situation.

I am now happy with myself and my ability to handle almost anything that life throws at me; if I feel lost again, all I have to do is find an adventure, point my bike in that direction and twist the throttle.

I understand the importance of "WoW factors" and "Moments." They are like jump-starters to our souls; I have seen so many "WoW Factors" and experienced so many "Moments" that I feel alive again, fully charged and ready to face whatever comes my way.

My bucket has been depleted of wishful content, which is excellent, but there's a bit of a void. I am looking at bigger dreams now, and the question is, how do I prepare for them? I still have to ride around Australia, but I also want to ride around New Zealand. I want to ride the Himalayas and possibly from Australia to England.

But I now realise that just riding around Australia is less interesting if you don't go to those out-of-the-way places and meet the people who live there. This means I will have to zigzag through each state and explore the history that is often overlooked. There's more of Queensland to see as well.

At the beginning of my adventure, I asked what Curley meant by his one-finger salute to the meaning of life. I believe it's pretty simple: Pick a dream, follow that dream, live that dream, and your mind will be free. When your mind is free, you will find satisfaction in life and peace with the world. Or, he could have been saying "Ein bier bitte" (one more beer please in crocodile language) "Prost".

I'm starting to form a new bucket list; there's an image forming about a ride through New South Wales, returning to where colonisation began in Australia. It was 1788 at a small, desolate harbour called Botany Bay, but it wasn't long until Sydney Cove was discovered. Australia became a nation within one hundred and twelve years; as they say, the rest is history.

I want to understand New South Wales, ride over the Sydney Harbour Bridge, ride along the side of the great Murray River and take a photo of Emu on the steps of the Opera House. For me, New South Wales is the old country; I have images of organised crime and prostitution at Kings Cross, the rise of unionism at the Rocks and of the killer funnel web spiders.

For now, this is just the end of the beginning of Emu's and my adventures throughout Australia. I hope this book has inspired you to pull items from your bucket list, assign a time frame to them, and make them a reality. If you see me on the road, remember that I like red wine and coffee! Ride safely.

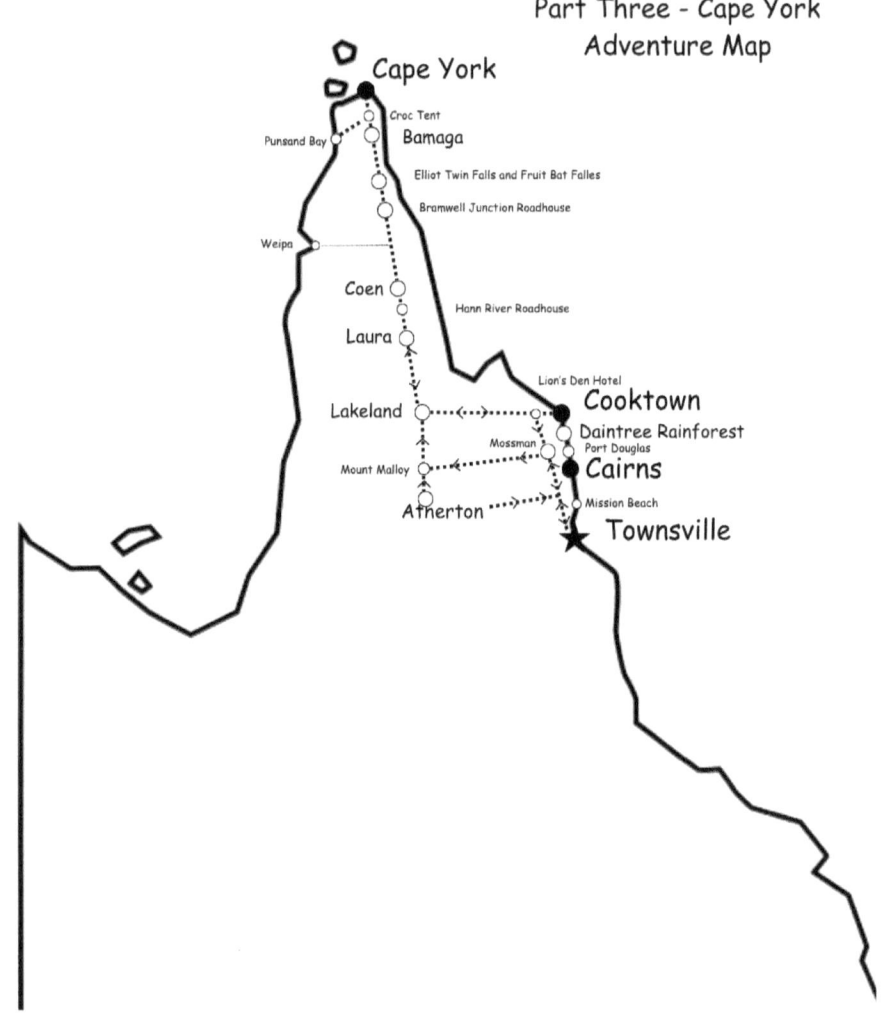

Giant termite mound near Bramwell Junction Roadhouse.

Five adventurers are ready for our attempt at Cape York. Atherton Caravan Park. We would meet Rob at the cafe in Atherton for breakfast.

Rob looks on as Flemming and Q fix Q's bike. Mount Malloy Rest Area.

Nick and Shayla are taking a break at Bob's Lookout on the Mulligan Highway.

Shayla is demonstrating a new dismount for adventure riders. Lakeland Roadhouse.

Flemming taking a break at the cultural centre in Laura.

Rob is checking his messages at Hann River Roadhouse—first night camping.

Nick camping on the first night - Hann River Roadhouse.

Quentin - Time for a beer. Hann River Roadhouse, Emu in the foreground.

The 'S' was added to the Exchange Hotel in Coen, by local tradies.

Bramwell Junction Roadhouse - Beginning of the Old Telegraph Track.

Group photo of a giant termite mound near the Bramwell Junction Roadhouse.

Bottomly Potts from Hairy MacClary's and Donaldson's Dairy. Ferocious guard dog.

Turn off to the southern section of the Old Telegraphy Track (OTT)

First creek crossing - Palm Creek

Nick and Shayla are waiting at the entry to the Northern Section of the Old Telegraph Track (OTT) and the entry to Fruit Bat Falls.

Nick is cooling off under the water at Fruit Bat Falls.

Rob and Shayla cooling off at Fruit Bat Falls.

Shayla modelling at the top of the falls.

Emu and I are riding down to the Jardine Ferry, hoping the Bamaga Road improves.

Punsand Bay Campground

Corrugations Bar - Punsand Bay Cape York

Carpark at the tip - Cape York

We made it to the northernmost point of the Australian continent - Cape York

Croc Tent - Cape York

Elliot Twin Falls - Northern Telegraph Track

Lions Den Hotel

Quentin and Rob are enjoying a beer at the Lion's Den Hotel.

Nick and Flemming on the Daintree Ferry on the journey home.

Assembled at the Mossman petrol station before we parted ways.

www.ingramcontent.com/pod-product-compliance
Lightning Source LLC
Chambersburg PA
CBHW060357080526
44583CB00012B/356